I0955672

HEALING YOUR GRIEVING HEART AFTER STILLBIRTH

Also by Alan Wolfelt:

Healing a Parent's Grieving Heart:
100 Practical Ideas After Your Child Dies

Healing a Child's Grieving Heart:
100 Practical Ideas for Families,
Friends and Caregivers

Healing a Friend's Grieving Heart:
100 Practical Ideas for Helping Someone
You Love Through Loss

Healing Your Grieving Heart for Kids:
100 Practical Ideas

The Journey Through Grief:
Reflections on Healing

Understanding Your Grief:
Ten Essential Touchstones for Finding
Hope and Healing Your Heart

The Wilderness of Grief: Finding Your Way

*Companion Press is dedicated to the education and
support of both the bereaved and bereavement caregivers.
We believe that those who companion the bereaved by
walking with them as they journey in grief have a
wondrous opportunity: to help others embrace and grow
through grief—and to lead fuller, more deeply-lived lives
themselves because of this important ministry.*

Companion
P R E S S

For a complete catalog and ordering information, write or call:

Companion Press
The Center for Loss and Life Transition
3735 Broken Bow Road
Fort Collins, CO 80526
(970) 226-6050
www.centerforloss.com

HEALING YOUR GRIEVING HEART AFTER STILLBIRTH

•

100 PRACTICAL IDEAS FOR PARENTS AND FAMILIES

•

ALAN D. WOLFELT, PH.D.
RAELYNN MALONEY, PH.D.

Companion
PRESS

Fort Collins, Colorado

An imprint of the Center for Loss and Life Transition

© 2013 by Alan D. Wolfelt, Ph.D.

Companion Press is an imprint of the
Center for Loss and Life Transition,
3735 Broken Bow Road, Fort Collins, Colorado 80526
970-226-6050
www.centerforloss.com

Companion Press books may be purchased in bulk for sales promotions, premiums or fundraisers. Please contact the publisher at the above address for more information.

Printed in the United States of America

22 21 20 19 18 17 16 15 14 13   5 4 3 2 1

ISBN: 978-1-61722-175-0

To the millions of hearts that have been torn apart by stillbirth. May you live and love wholly again while always remembering your precious baby who died.

CONTENTS

INTRODUCTION

Your precious baby has died. It's as if a deep hole has imploded inside of you. The hole penetrates you and leaves you gasping for air. You are in mourning. You are "bereaved," and this literally means "to be torn apart" and "to have special needs." We are truly sorry for your loss.

The stillbirth of your precious daughter or son is an inexplicable loss of hopes and dreams of a new life—to you as parents, to the siblings this baby may have, to your extended family, and to your friends. The impact of this overwhelming loss is profound and life-changing.

People sometimes ask us why stillbirth is so different from other death losses. The grieving parents we have been honored to "companion" have taught us that few events in life bring about such warm and wonderful feelings of anticipation as the announcement of a pregnancy. As soon as you and your family learn you are expecting, you naturally begin to have hopes and dreams for the future. These hopes and dreams take on a life of their own and begin to grow inside you, even as your baby is growing.

Yet when you come to grief and are "torn apart," there is no longer a living baby to go with your hopes and dreams. You have come to grief before you were prepared to mourn.

More than two million babies are stillborn worldwide each year, about one in 160 pregnancies. Each baby's death is a tragedy. Most of the time the baby dies before labor begins, but sometimes the baby dies during labor (about 15 percent). These numbers represent many, many millions of people across the world who have been affected by stillbirth and whose grieving hearts are crying out for expression and support. As you're reading, regardless of these statistics, your thoughts naturally go to your unique child.

Stillbirth is defined as the death of a baby before or during birth who has reached at least 20 weeks' gestation (some countries use 24 weeks, others 28 weeks). The death of a baby before that time is technically considered a miscarriage. But we know, as you do, that no matter how many weeks or months pregnant you were when you learned your precious baby died, you grieve and you need to mourn. The heart knows no magic number and often begins bonding very early in pregnancy. Actually, as you know, attachment to your "wished-for child" begins even prior to conception. So if your baby died before or during birth and you seek compassionate support for your grief, this book is for you.

We'd also like to acknowledge that some people may read this book in the window of time after they have learned their baby has died but before the baby has been delivered. If you are among them, we encourage you to read through this book and know that you have the right to begin to mourn your loss and to spend time with your precious baby after delivery. Seeing, holding, photographing, and saying goodbye to your baby often helps grieving parents in the difficult weeks and months ahead. As we often say, you first have to say hello on any pathway to goodbye.

Sadly, it has only been in recent years that a family's grief over a stillborn baby has been acknowledged as a significant loss by our society. Even today, many people around you do not know what to say or do to provide you with support and comfort. In addition, there are no cultural norms for mourning the loss of someone who has never lived outside the womb and was never formally welcomed into your larger community of family and friends.

In their lack of knowledge of how to support you, well-meaning friends and even family members may make your experience even more difficult through some things they say and do. Someone will invariably imply that the loss of a pregnancy isn't serious or overwhelming because "you can have another one." Someone is bound to say things like, "You didn't really get to know the baby" or "It's probably for the best...maybe he or she was going to have a difficult life." Yet, you may have seen your lovely baby on an ultrasound and heard her heart beat and felt her movements inside of you....all ways of getting to know your unique child.

In the name of faith, some people project theologized clichés like, "God wouldn't give you any more than you can bear" or "God must have needed him more than you did" or the dreadful "Now you have an angel in Heaven." Of course, all you can think about is wanting your child here where he belongs, in your loving arms.

Some people also indulge in their own illusion of needing to control this painful experience by suggesting that the outcome could have been prevented by different medical care or something the mother should have or could have done. These blaming and shaming comments, however wrongheaded they may be, often hurt and fuel any feelings of anger, guilt, or regret that you may carry inside.

Yes, the type of death you have experienced creates so many natural complications for your mourning.

Perhaps your most important "special need" right now is to be compassionate with yourself. The word compassion literally means "with passion." So, self-compassion means caring for oneself "with passion." While we hope you have excellent outside support, this little book is intended to help you be kind to yourself as you confront and eventually embrace your grief over the death of your baby.

Over our years of walking with people in grief, we have discovered that many of us are hard on ourselves when we are in mourning. We often have inappropriate expectations of how "well" we should be doing with our grief. These expectations result from common societal messages that tell us to be strong in the face of grief. We are told to "carry on," to "keep your chin up," and to "keep busy." In actuality, when we are in grief we need to slow down, turn inward, embrace our feelings of loss, as well as seek and accept support. It's a challenge to be self-compassionate in our mourning-avoiding culture.

But good self-care is essential to your survival. To practice good self-care and self-compassion doesn't mean you are feeling sorry for yourself; rather, it means you are allowing yourself to heal. For it is in nurturing ourselves, in allowing ourselves the time and loving attention we need to journey through our grief, that we find meaning in our continued living. It is in having the courage to care for our own needs that we discover a fullness to living and loving again.

We hope the words we express from our hearts throughout the following pages bring you some solace. We realize that no book can make your overwhelming loss go away. It rages in the recesses of your soul. Your profound loss will endure, and nothing we can say or do will alter that truth.

Yes, you have a broken heart. We truly believe that acknowledging your heart is broken is the beginning of your healing. As you experience the pain of your loss—gently opening, acknowledging, and allowing—the suffering it has wrought diminishes but never completely vanishes. In fact, the resistance to the pain can potentially be more painful than the pain itself. Running from the pain of loss closes down our hearts and spirits. As difficult as it is, we must relinquish ourselves to the pain of grief. As Helen Keller said, "The only way to the other side is through."

Yet going through the pain of loss is not in and of itself the goal in our grief journeys. Instead, it is rediscovering life in ways that give us reason to get our feet out of bed and to make life matter. We're certain you realize that the death of your baby is not something you will ever "overcome" or "let go of." The death of your baby doesn't call out to be "cured," "resolved," or "explained" but to be experienced. This experience is a kind of "enforced learning in your life." If anyone inappropriately tells you that "you will grow from this," remember the word ENFORCED. This is not a growth experience you would choose.

As promised, this book contains 100 practical ideas to help you practice self-compassion. Some of the ideas will teach you about the principles of grief and mourning. One of the most important ways to help yourself is to learn about the grief experience; the more you know, the less likely you will be to unknowingly perpetuate some of our society's harmful myths about grief and healing.

The remainder of the 100 ideas offer practical, here-and-now, action-oriented tips for embracing your grief. Each idea is followed by a brief explanation of how and why the idea might help you.

You'll also notice that each of the 100 ideas suggests a *carpe diem*, which means, as fans of the movie *Dead Poets Society* will remember, "seize the day." Our hope is that you will not relegate this book to your shelves but keep it handy on your nightstand or desk. Pick it up often and turn to any page; the *carpe diem* suggestion will help you seize the day by helping you move toward healing today, right now, right this minute. If you come to an idea that doesn't seem to fit you, ignore it and flip to a different page.

Our sincere hope is that this little book will give you some solace and hope for your healing. May you discover courage in places both obvious and hidden along the way. May you stay present to your grief and not turn away but be filled with a commitment to see what it has to say. May you hold hope, courage, and faith high like candles in the dark and bravely walk forward, even when everything inside of you urges you to turn and run away.

Bless you. We hope to meet you one day.

Alan Wolfelt   Raelynn Maloney

1.

MOURN THE LOSS OF YOUR PRECIOUS BABY

*"There is no foot so small that it cannot
leave an imprint on this world."*
— Unknown

- Everyone grieves when someone we love dies, but if we are to heal our grief, we must also mourn.

- Your body and mind's natural response to your baby's death is to grieve. Grief is the constellation of internal thoughts and feelings you have when you lose someone you have come to love and value.

- Your grief is what you may experience as a weight in the chest, a churning in your stomach, an ache in your arms, a memory of being told that your baby was not going to take his or her first breath, or a recollection of the moment you held your stillborn baby in your arms.

- Mourning, on the other hand, is the outward expression of your grief. It is an active process. Mourning is releasing your grief, be it through tears, writing your thoughts in a journal, creating art that represents your feelings of grief, writing out lyrics to a song that describes your heartache, talking to others about your baby, or telling the story of the life and death.

- Many of the ideas in this book are intended to help you mourn the death of your precious baby. These ideas have been written to help you express your grief outside of yourself so that over time your heart can heal.

CARPE DIEM:

Check in with yourself and ask, "Am I allowing myself to actively mourn my baby's death, or am I holding my grief inside?"

2.

KNOW THAT NUMBNESS IS NATURAL

"Sorrow comes in great waves...but rolls over us, and though it may almost smother us, it leaves us. And we know that if it is strong, we are stronger, inasmuch as it passes and we remain."
— Henry James

- During the first hours, days, and weeks after your baby's death, you are likely to feel shock, emotional numbness, and disbelief that any of this is real.

- These feelings are nature's way of temporarily protecting you from feeling overwhelmed by the full reality of the death. Like anesthesia, they help you survive the pain of your early grief. Numbness is natural and necessary early in your grief process.

- What does numbness feel like? You may feel mentally foggy. Or you may find yourself thinking, "I will wake up from this and it will not have happened." When we first begin to mourn a loss, it can feel like being in a dream. Your emotions will need to catch up with what your mind had been told.

- Numbness can also be experienced as a desire to be more passive in your day. You may not feel like taking care of yourself in basic ways or doing only what is absolutely necessary. You may want to be led through the day a bit so that you don't have to think or make choices. You may need others to make even simple decisions for you. You may move a little more slowly through your day or feel less productive than normal. This slowing down is a natural need your body and mind have so that you can begin to take in the reality of the loss.

- Even after you have moved beyond these initial feelings of numbness and begin to feel more clearheaded, don't be surprised if they reemerge later, further into your grief journey. Birthdays, holidays, and anniversaries often trigger normal and necessary feelings of numbness.

CARPE DIEM

Give yourself permission to take a time-out from making decisions right now. Cancel any activities that demand concentration or focus so that you can allow your mind and body to heal before putting them to work again.

3.

UNDERSTAND THE SIX NEEDS OF MOURNING

Need #1. Acknowledge the reality of the death

"Grief is a process of awareness, of making real inside the self an event that already occurred in reality outside."
— Parkes and Weiss

- Your baby has died. This is probably the most difficult reality in the world to accept. Your mind and heart will try hard to push this reality away. This is normal and necessary for your survival. Yet gently, slowly, patiently over time you will begin to embrace this reality. Little by little. Hour by hour. You will come to integrate the reality in doses as you are ready.

- Whether your beautiful baby died because of something that occurred suddenly or the death was anticipated, acknowledging the full reality of the loss will happen as time passes. Over the coming months and years there will be many experiences that will remind you of this reality. These are necessary experiences for you to have, as painful as they may be.

- You will first acknowledge the reality of the loss with your head, and then, over time, you will begin to acknowledge the emotional reality with your heart and soul.

CARPE DIEM

Tell someone about your baby today. Talk about how you decided to name her or what it was like to first see her.

4.

UNDERSTAND THE SIX NEEDS OF MOURNING

Need #2. Embrace the Pain of the Loss

"We must embrace pain and burn it as fuel for our journey."
— Kenji Miyazawa

- Embracing pain may be furthest from your mind right now. In fact, you are more likely to be actively finding ways to avoid or prevent yourself from feeling the pain of this loss day in and day out. Embracing pain is something we naturally do not want to do. It is easier to avoid, repress, or push away the pain of grief than it is to confront it and feel through it.

- Confronting and allowing your pain to surface is what will help you reconcile and integrate the reality that this is not a baby you will raise, because he died before birth.

- In the early days after the death, the pain often feels ever-present, as if it doesn't let up for even a moment. During this early time, you will probably need to seek refuge from your pain for periods of time. You simply cannot take in the enormity of your loss all at once. It's healthy to seek distractions and allow yourself bits of pleasure everyday. Go for a walk, watch television, or talk to friends about something other than death.

- After some time has passed, you will find that the sorrow you feel surfaces less often. While you may enjoy the reprieve, it is important for you to find ways to consciously invite your pain to resurface, feel through it, and continue to integrate it.

CARPE DIEM

Dedicate 10 minutes to thinking and feeling about the loss. If you don't want to be alone for this, reach out to someone who doesn't try to stop your tears or take your pain away with words. Sit with this person as you express how painful this experience is for you.

5.

UNDERSTAND THE SIX NEEDS OF MOURNING

Need #3. Remember the Baby Who Died

"As long as I can, I will look at this world for both of us. As long as I can I will laugh with the birds, I will sing with the flowers, I will pray to the stars, for both of us."

—Sascha

- To heal in grief, it is important to remember your baby and commemorate this precious being whose life ended much too soon.

- If those around you try to take memories away from you in a misguided attempt to spare you from more pain, express to them that this is not helpful to your grief. It is good for you to share or display photos of your baby, even photos of the baby after she died. It is good to talk about your daughter, both happy and sad memories of your pregnancy as well as her birth and death. It is good to cherish a blanket or item of clothing that touched your daughter's precious body before you had to say goodbye.

- In the early weeks and months of your grief, you may fear that you will forget her. The details of her face, her smell, the feel of her skin. Rest assured that while time may blur some of your memories, as you slowly shift your relationship from one of presence to one of memory, the moments you shared with her will be imprinted in your memory.

- Remind yourself that it is remembering the past that makes hoping for the future possible.

CARPE DIEM

If you took photos of your daughter or son, copy the pictures and make a special photo album for yourself, your partner, and each of your kids. On each page write down something you remember about wanting to have a baby, about your pregnancy, or about your feelings of love on the day you got to see your baby.

6.

UNDERSTAND THE SIX NEEDS OF MOURNING

Need #4. Develop a New Self-Identity

"Identity is such a crucial affair that one shouldn't rush into it."
—David Quammen

- A big part of your self-identity was formed by the relationship you had with your daughter or son. Yes, you and your baby had a relationship even before he was born. This relationship began the moment you began to think about having a baby.

- You have gone from being a parent to-be to being a bereaved parent. You are the mother or father to this sweet child. If this was your only child, you may wonder whether his death means that you are a parent at all. Even if you have other children, your baby's death will alter your perception of who you are as a parent in many ways.

- While you must work through this difficult need, we can assure you that you are and always will be your child's parent. From the moment you discovered you were going to be parents to a new baby, you walked through a door that can never be closed.

- Re-anchor yourself so your feet are on solid ground as you embark on this journey to reconstruct your self-identity. This involves exploring and redefining what it means to be a parent and a family now that one precious member is not physically present in your everyday life.

CARPE DIEM

Work on articulating how this loss is changing you. Using the following, complete the sentences with the words that feel right to you. I used to be _____. Now that _____died, I am _____. When I used to think about _____, I felt _____. Today, when I think about _____, I feel _____. Keeping writing as long as you want.

7.

UNDERSTAND THE SIX
NEEDS OF MOURNING

Need #5. Search for Meaning

"In some ways suffering ceases to be suffering at the moment it finds a meaning, such as the meaning of a sacrifice."
— Viktor E. Frankl

• When a baby dies, it feels so unnatural and out of order. This death violates nature and the order of the universe. We naturally question the meaning and purpose of this sad turn of events. No question is too small or too strange. All of them are important questions to ask. Why did my child die before me? Why does a baby die before he is even born? What is the point in that?

• "Why" questions may surface uncontrollably and often precede "how" questions. This mental quandary that occurs with grief can feel consuming at times. You might be asking, "Why did this happen? How much pain can one person endure? How will my life be different? How will it be the same?"

• Remember that having faith or spirituality does not eliminate your need to mourn. Even if you believe in an afterlife of some kind, you and your child have still lost precious time together here on earth. It's normal to feel dumbfounded and angry at God or whatever source within the universe you may believe has permitted this to happen.

• Ultimately, you may decide that there is no answer to the question of "Why did this happen?" For some parents the only answer is this: My baby dying before birth does not make sense and it never will.

CARPE DIEM

Start a list of "why" questions that have surfaced for you.
Find a friend or counselor who will help you find your own
answers, and explore (not tritely answer) these questions
with you. Ask your spouse or children to do the same.

8.

UNDERSTAND THE SIX NEEDS OF MOURNING

Need #6. Receive Ongoing Support From Others

"You must be at the end of your rope. I felt a tug."
— Unknown

• As mourners we need the love and understanding of others as we move through our grief toward healing.

• Unfortunately, our society places too much value on "carrying on" and "doing well" after a death. So many mourners are abandoned by their friends and family soon after the death. This is especially true in stillbirth because many do not understand that it is a significant and painful loss. Often family and friends avoid encounters because they don't know what to say.

• Keep in mind the rule of thirds: one third of your friends will be supportive of your need to mourn, one third will make you feel worse, and one third will neither help nor hinder.

• Grief is experienced in doses over years, not quickly and efficiently. As you encounter your pain, you will need the continued support of your friends and family for weeks and months and years to come. If you are not getting the support you need most, be sure to ask for it. Usually people are more than willing to help, but they don't know what to do or what not to do. You may have to practice being assertive and up front about what help would benefit you right now.

CARPE DIEM

Make a list of the things that would be helpful for others to take care of. Send an email or a text to your three closest friends letting them know that these are a few of the things that would help you the most right now. Asking for help is hard, but practicing this is vital as you move through your grief.

9.

KNOW THERE IS NO ORDER TO GRIEF

*"Serenity is not freedom from the storm,
but peace amid the storm."*

– Unknown

- Grief is anything but orderly and predictable. You are not going to move through a series of stages toward some particular end point. If you can, consider your grief a journey, not a destination.

- Though the needs of mourning are numbered 1 through 6 in the previous pages, it's important to know that grief is not an ordered progression toward hope and healing. Don't fall into the trap of thinking your grief journey will be predictable or always forward-moving. Mourning is really a process that unfolds in its own unique way depending on how you choose to express yourself.

- Usually, grief hurts more before it begins to hurt less. Sometimes it will feel as if you are taking two steps forward and one step back.

- You will probably experience a multitude of different emotions in a wave-like fashion. You will also likely be working on more than one need of mourning at a time. This is normal.

- Be compassionate with yourself as you experience your own unique grief journey.

CARPE DIEM

If you have read about or been told about the "stages" of grief, remember this is not how your grief will unfold. Don't allow yourself or others to tell you how, when, and what your grief will be like. It will unfold in its own unique way.

10.

IF YOU DECIDED NOT TO SEE YOUR BABY AFTER BIRTH, FIND OTHER WAYS TO ACKNOWLEDGE THE REALITY OF THE DEATH

"The body is a sacred garment."

— Martha Graham

- When a baby is stillborn, parents and other family members sometimes choose not to see the baby's body. Perhaps this was a choice you made, or perhaps you were not given a choice and left the hospital without having time with your baby.

- Never viewing the baby's body can complicate your grief. You may struggle with accepting the reality of the death. Your mind may be more prone to get stuck on the question, "Is she really dead? Did she really die at birth?" You may wonder if the baby who was buried or cremated was really your baby (despite all objective evidence to the contrary). And you may worry about whether your baby is being taken care of and wonder if perhaps there is still a chance that she will be returned to you.

- Our minds can cope with what they know, but they cannot cope with what's been kept from them. If you weren't able to see and hold your baby's body after death, it will be important for you to find other ways to confront the reality that the baby died. Maybe it would help to read the autopsy report or to have someone read it for you and tell you in layman's terms what it says. If photos were taken by anyone and you feel ready, you may want to view them with a trusted friend or family member. You could also talk to your doctor or the funeral home staff who cared for your baby's body after death.

CARPE DIEM

Talk to someone you trust about never having seen the body. Acknowledging the reality of the death is a vital part of your grief journey, and you may have strong feelings about not having been given space, time, or encouragement to be with your baby's body. Sometimes just giving voice to this loss can be very powerful.

11.

PRACTICE SELF-COMPASSION

*"Sometimes the purpose of a day is to merely feel
our sadness, knowing that as we do, we allow whole
layers of grief, like old skin cells, to drop off us."*

— Marianne Williamson

- Be compassionate with yourself as you move throughout your days. At first, the painful thoughts and feelings may feel ever-present, a constant in your mind. There may be experiences, objects, or statements made by others that trigger painful emotions. Allow yourself to express these emotions when they are triggered. Cry, scream, write, or talk openly with someone who can simply listen without advising or explaining.

- Allow yourself to think, feel, and do whatever you need to think, feel, and do to survive early on. Try to keep the judgments about how or what you are doing to a minimum. There is no specific way you are "supposed" to grieve, so when you find yourself saying, "I'm supposed to be angry," take a moment to remind yourself that what you are feeling is exactly what you are supposed to be feeling. Give yourself permission to grieve *your* way. There is no single right way to grieve, no orderly stages you will go through, and absolutely no timetable.

- If others judge you or try to direct your grief in ways that seem unhelpful or even hurtful, remind yourself that there is only one person who knows what is best. You are the only expert of your grief. You can choose to believe what they say, or you can believe in your own intuitive grief process. Others are often well-intentioned but may lack insight about how stillbirth loss impacts a person physically, mentally, emotionally, and spiritually. If you can, have compassion for their attempt to provide support, even if it did not feel supportive to you.

CARPE DIEM

Instead of pushing yourself to do more, dedicate a time
every day to being still. Do nothing but take care of yourself
in some small way—get a massage, take a long shower,
watch a comedy, eat something that you love to eat.

12.

BE COMPASSIONATE WITH YOUR PARTNER

*"If you want others to be happy, practice compassion.
If you want to be happy, practice compassion."*
— the Dalai Lama

- Unless you are widowed or a single parent, your baby's other parent is probably also mired in grief.

- Because your experiences with this loss are so different from one another's, you may not recognize your partner's behaviors or emotions as grief. Be as compassionate and nonjudgmental as you can about your partner's reactions to the death. Don't debate with one another about whose recollection is more accurate or which of you is feeling more pain.

- As a mother, you may feel more affected by the death. In fact, some research has shown that a mother's grief is more disabling and longer-lasting. This may be in part because you carried and took care of this child in ways that fathers are not given the opportunity to. Women also tend to be more outwardly emotional and slower to return to daily routines than men. It's important not to compare your grief, however, because your experiences with the baby were not the same.

- Fathers often feel the same depth of grief when their baby dies, though these feelings can go unexpressed because society expects men to be "stronger." Men often appear to be more stoic, and they may want to return to work faster. That being said, it is also important to know that in some marriages these roles are reversed. All these responses are normal and are not a gauge of the parent's love for the baby.

- The intensity of one's grief depends on many factors, including how and when the baby died, how engaged each parent was in the pregnancy, how the process of delivering the baby went, how supportive the staff at the hospital were, and how much support is available to you now.

CARPE DIEM

Take 10 minutes today to sit down with your partner. Talk with one another without accusing or judging. Look at each other, connect by holding each other's hands, and talk about any unreconciled feelings you have toward him or her regarding the death.

13.

BE LOVING TOWARD YOUR SURVIVING CHILDREN

*"There is something you must always remember.
You are braver than you believe, stronger than
you seem, and smarter than you think."*
—Winnie the Pooh

• If you have other children, they too are experiencing the pain of this loss in their own unique way. Grieving siblings are often "forgotten mourners." This means that parents, extended family, friends, and society tend to overlook that they have also lost someone they love.

• Siblings may not express grief directly and, instead, indirectly demonstrate to others that they are struggling. They may show some regressive behaviors, like wanting to sleep with mom and dad, clinging to parents more often, or asking to be taken care of in ways they were when they were younger. They may also display sadness, anger, or anxiety through behaviors such as irritability, blame, distractibility, decreased motivation at school, and disorganization. If supportive grown-ups can help grieving siblings find more direct and healthy ways of coping, these indirect expressions of grief may go away.

• What grieving siblings need is for adults to be open and honest with them about the death. They need to know that it is okay to talk about the baby by name and about the baby's death. They need to be reassured that their grief is important too. They need their unique thoughts and feelings acknowledged by others.

• Pay attention to how much your grief consumes your household day in and day out. Your children have daily needs—school, activities, nutrition, hygiene, social events. Your home should still be a sanctuary for your children.

CARPE DIEM

Gather together as a family in a comfortable room in the house.
Go around and have each person share how he or she is feeling
since the baby died. You may uncover some new memories, fears,
or questions that you didn't know were present in the house.

18

14.

RELEASE YOUR TEARS

*"Tears have a wisdom all their own. They come when
a person has relaxed enough to let go and to work
through his sorrow. They are the natural bleeding
of an emotional wound, carrying the poison out
of the system. Here lies the road to recovery."*

— F. Alexander Magoun

- Why allow yourself to cry? Tears are your body's way of naturally cleansing and healing itself. After someone we love dies, we naturally feel hurt, helpless, and vulnerable. Your tears are an expression of these feelings. Tears communicate to those around you (and to yourself) that you are carrying pain and it needs release. Through your tears your grief moves from the inside out.

- If you are not crying a lot, that is OK too. The inability or lack of tears is not a deficit in you. It may simply mean that you are still experiencing shock or disbelief about the death. Or you may be finding other ways to move your grief from the inside to the outside. If you are unsure of how others will respond to your tears, this may also keep you from releasing them. Please tell yourself that tears are actually a reminder that you are a human being who has the capacity to give and receive love. Your human heart is feeling torn apart by the loss of this beautiful baby you came to love.

- You may find that those around you are uncomfortable with your tears. Often others do not know what to say when you cry. They may inadvertently try to stop your tears from flowing, telling you "It'll be all right." As a society we're often not so good at witnessing others in pain. Express to your friends and family that you need to cry right now and that they can help you most by allowing you to cry as often, as loudly, and as embarrassingly as you need to.

CARPE DIEM

Find a place where you know you can allow yourself to cry—
in your car, in the shower, into your pillow, in the arms of
someone you love. Take time today to release some of the
tears. Cry as long and as hard as your body needs.

15.

DESIGNATE A TIME TO MOURN EACH DAY

*"Many people are alive but don't touch
the miracle of being alive."*
— Thich Nhat Hanh

- Mourning is exhausting work. It is often something that we try hard to prevent, avoid, or deny.

- In an effort to move toward your grief rather than away from it, consider making mourning part of your daily routine. When it hurts, you know mourning is working. It is helping you process and transform your grief. Just like the other ways that you take care of yourself—taking a shower, eating a good meal, going for a walk—mourning is a way of taking care of your grieving self.

- Set aside a quiet time each day, even if it is only five minutes. Use this time to consciously embrace your thoughts and feelings about the death, which may be constantly there anyway.

- The first ten minutes after you wake up might be a good time to do this, like a release of emotion prior to entering the day. This also might be a good time to journal about what surfaces.

- Creating a dedicated mourning time may allow you to concentrate on truly living rather than merely existing as you move through the rest of your day.

CARPE DIEM

Conscious mourning sounds absurd, we know. Consciously invite pain into my day? Yes, it will come into your day without warning anyway because it demands to be seen and heard. The more time you spend consciously inviting it, the less time there is for your sorrow to surface without warning.

16.

ACKNOWLEDGE THAT
YOU ARE A PARENT

*"You don't really understand human nature unless
you know why a child on a merry-go-round will
wave at his parents every time around—and
why his parents will always wave back."*

—William D. Tammeuson

- When a baby who is an only child is stillborn, many parents question whether or not this means they are parents anymore. If you have other children, you may wonder if you are still a parent to this baby who died. Can you be a parent to a child who is not living?

- Ironically, we call children who lose their parents orphans and spouses who lose their partner widows or widowers, but we have no name for parents when their child dies.

- Be assured you are still very much a parent and yes, you are the parents to your baby. You were parents from the moment you began to feel like a parent (for some this is at conception). You were a parent from the day your connection to and hopes for this baby began to take shape.

- If you are the baby's mother, you carried your baby for months, and the things you did during this time were indeed parenting. If you are the newborn's father, you also were parenting any time you talked to your baby or helped nurture your wife as she carried your child.

CARPE DIEM

Do you question your status as a parent? Take a moment to
reflect on the ways that you "parented" this baby in the ways
that you could while your baby was in utero. Talk with your
partner about how the two of you loved and parented this
baby during the pregnancy to remind yourselves that parenting
begins long before a baby is physically present in this world.

17.

UNDERSTAND WHEN OTHERS SAY, "I'M SORRY"

"Apology is a lovely perfume; it can transform the clumsiest moment into a gracious gift."

— Margaret Lee Runbeck

- Many bereaved parents share that the words they find most unhelpful are when others say, "I'm sorry." Those words somehow lose their meaning when they are said too often.

- You may wonder what they are sorry for. After all, they were not responsible for this tragedy. You may think, "I don't need you to be sorry. I need you to wrap your arms around me so that I know I am not alone right now."

- If you are wondering what you are supposed to say in response to the common utterance "I'm sorry," perhaps it would help if you knew what the person actually means to say: "I'm sorry that you are going through this pain and there is nothing I can do to take it away."

- Before your baby died, perhaps you yourself offered this compassionate response to another human being mired in grief—a friend, a parent, your partner, or one of your children. Indeed, there is nothing anyone can say or do to take away the pain because the pain in a necessary part of loss. With the loss of someone or something we love, we naturally feel pain. It is a necessary part of the journey.

CARPE DIEM

Think about how you would like to respond to the next person who tells you she is sorry. Would you like to acknowledge, "I know you are sorry that I am going through this. Thank you for saying that"? Or would you simply like to remind yourself that this is what they mean, then accept those two words with more open arms?

18.

JUST BE

*"The western mind is obsessed by doing more
and more, restless and constantly on the run, just
cannot sit still into being the grace that descends…
just by being…still, being leads to being."*

— Swami Rajneesh

- Here is a real challenge for you: Drop all of your plans and obligations for today and do nothing.

- Another way to just "be" is to practice some form of meditation. Meditation can help center you, slow down your racing thoughts, and relax your physical body. Meditation is simply quiet, relaxed contemplation. You need not follow any particular rules or techniques although learning proper ways of breathing can help you gain a deeper state of stillness. Simply find a place where you can focus on whatever flows in and out of your mind. When you are distracted by noises, people, or tasks, just bring your mind back to your breath. This may take some practice!

- Find someplace quiet, be still, close your eyes, and focus on breathing in and out. Listen to your breath. Notice your muscles relaxing as you breathe tension out with each out-breath. Perhaps you will find such stillness that you will be able to hear your own heartbeat. If in this moment your mind wanders to thoughts of your newborn, allow yourself to have the thought and then move your attention back to your breath.

CARPE DIEM

Sit down and hold something soft in your hands (a pair of socks
or a soft ball, for example). Focus on just feeling the object and
take 10 deep breaths. Breathe in and fill your belly with your
inhale (rather than filling your chest). Then, slightly slower
than when you breathed in, let the air out of your belly.

19.

OPEN YOUR HEART

*"I've learned that whenever I decide something with
an open heart, I usually make the right decision."*
— Maya Angelou

- When we experience loss, our first response is almost always to close ourselves off, to protect our heart and soul from experiencing more pain. We sometimes will even find ourselves guarded or closed off from the people we love the most—our partner, our surviving children, our parents.

- Opening your heart can be difficult when you have experienced such a painful loss. But it is not impossible. Perhaps through meditation you can visualize your open heart, or through yoga you can embody your open heart through poses that open your chest. If you do not practice meditation or yoga, try sitting and using your imagination to make space in your heart, enough space to let at least one person in for right now. You can continue to work on expanding this, but opening to even one person right now is a good start.

- Open hearts allow love to flow in as well as out.

CARPE DIEM

Try reflecting on this thought: "As I allow myself to mourn,
I create an opening in my heart. Releasing the tensions of
grief, surrendering to the struggle, means freeing myself to
go forward and allowing myself to love and to be loved."

20.

REMEMBER: ONE DAY AT A TIME

*"Enjoy the little things, for one day you may look
back and realize they were the big things."*
— Robert Brault

- Powerful emotions stemming from grief may lead you to believe you will never be happy again, or at least not as happy as you were. It's important to acknowledge those emotions and this belief that feels so true to you right now.

- It's equally important to remind yourself that despite how you feel at this moment, you will continue to grow and live one breath at a time.

- If you focus on being able to take one breath in and one breath out, and then one hour at a time, and then one day at a time, with loving support and time you will again experience joy. The joy you feel may not be the same, you are right about that. Why? Because having your baby die at birth changes you. You are not the same person you were before this experience, and part of your grief journey is getting reacquainted with your new self.

- Resuming normal daily activities will help you on your journey to renew your commitment to life. Try not to lose your self in your work or in the rapid flow of life demands. At the beginning of each day, take note that it is a new day and that new opportunities await you.

CARPE DIEM

It is important to reestablish structure in your days when you feel ready. Make a checklist of what you need to do and then prioritize what needs to be done. Check off what you complete. Try immersing yourself and be present in each activity, even if it's only for a few minutes. Use your breath to anchor you into the present moment throughout the day.

21.

UNDERSTAND WHAT IT MEANS TO BE "TRAUMATIZED"

"Sometimes a breakdown can be the beginning of a kind of breakthrough, a way of living in advance through a trauma that prepares you for a future of radical transformation."

— Cherrie Moraga

- The death of a baby in utero is usually a sudden, unexpected death, and for some parents who experience stillbirth, the death is traumatic. Perhaps the baby died during birth, or perhaps the baby died as a result of someone or something violently causing harm to the pregnancy. If your baby died because of trauma to the mother (as a result of being abused at the hands of another, a car accident, or an invasive medical procedure for example), these experiences will result in traumatic grief.

- If you've been traumatized by a sudden death, it is important to know that your grief will be different than the grief that results from an anticipated death. As you know, the death of someone loved always causes painful feelings, but in the case of a sudden, violent death, your mind has an especially difficult time acknowledging and absorbing the circumstances of the death itself.

- Certainly it can be said that death is always traumatic. Even the natural death of an elderly parent can feel traumatic to her children. But sudden, violent death results in a kind of psychic injury and typically involves frightening and often intrusive thoughts about the distressful event that caused the death.

CARPE DIEM

If you have grieved the death of someone loved before, consider how your feelings may be different this time. How is the traumatic nature of your baby's death shaping your grief right now?

22.

SEEK SAFETY AND COMFORT

"Remember, we all stumble, every one of us. That's
why it's a comfort to go hand-in-hand."
— Emily Kimbrough

- Birthing a stillborn baby can be a traumatic experience for a couple. This is not how you expected the labor and delivery to be. You may even have had to anticipate this day for the past week or two, waiting for the delivery after being told that your baby is no longer alive inside of you. For you, the physical pain of labor and delivery was also wrought with emotional pain. On the other side of the birthing experience was not the same joyous experience you imagined— holding your tiny living, breathing newborn baby in your arms.

- After a traumatic experience, it's natural to feel vulnerable, restless, and anxious. Your nervous system is telling your brain that the world is not the safe, loving place that you thought it was and that you long for it to be right now. Your brain was anticipating the birth to be a safe, loving experience and it was not.

- To overcome your trauma, you must locate yourself among people and in places that make you feel safe. If this means having your doctor check your vitals in the hospital or get your blood tested to assure you that your body is functioning properly, that's OK. If this means avoiding certain places or people, that's OK too. If your anxiety becomes overwhelming and you feel the need to do things that may purely be anxiety-driven, such as having your other children receive a physical to be sure they're fine, you may want to find someone to talk with to help you find ways to reestablish your sense of safety and security.

CARPE DIEM

When we are anxious it helps to feel taken care of. Let
someone else take care of you today. It's normal and
natural to need help with the activities of daily living in
the early days and weeks after a traumatic death.

23.

MAKE AN INVENTORY OF SURVIVAL STRATEGIES

"We need 4 hugs a day for survival. We need 8 hugs a day for maintenance. We need 12 hugs a day for growth."
— Virginia Satir

- Survival is one step followed by the next... followed by the next. What has helped you cope with stress and loss in the past? These strategies will probably help you now too.

- Each of us has coping skills that we have used in times of distress. Sometimes our coping strategies are effective and healthy; other times we fall back on them simply because they are what is familiar to us. They have worked "well enough" that we continue to return to them when we are struggling.

- Make a list of the most difficult times in your life and the ways in which you helped yourself live through them. Did you spend time with family? Write? Turn to your faith? Help take care of someone else? Which activities calm you? Getting a massage, talking a walk, going for a swim, talking to your sister on the phone, walking the dog, reading a book, meditating? These are the survival techniques that you want to try to use today and every day.

- Make note of any of these that are unhealthy ways of managing your suffering, such as substance abuse, gambling, or overeating, for example. We want to be sure these are not the coping skills you turn to during this difficult time.

CARPE DIEM

Make a list of what you need to get through the next week. This could include more time alone, more time with others, daily tasks that are hanging over your head, or something you really want to do but don't have the capacity to plan right now. Looking ahead a week at a time may seem less overwhelming than thinking about months or the next year. Ask your friends and family to help if your list contains items that you are well aware you will not be able to do on your own.

24.

BE PATIENT

---

*"When we lose those we love, you must understand
that it takes time to learn to feel again. For nothing
can touch the heart which is frozen with grief."*

— Unknown

• I'm sure you've realized by now that healing in grief does not happen quickly. Remember, grief is not something we truly ever "get over." You will spend a lifetime continuing to integrate this loss into your being and someday, instead of carrying the heavy, compressing, painful grief you may feel right now, you will carry your integrated grief. When grief is integrated, your loss will still be a part of you but it will not weigh or slow you down.

• In our hurried North American culture, patience can be especially hard to find. It's a behavior that is becoming less and less commonplace, as we are all rushing around and trying to do everything at once.

• Yet patience, not urgency, is vital in grief. Our grief will not heed anyone's timetable—including our own. Be patient with your body, mind, and spirit. Be patient with those around you if they are not where you want them to be in their own grief. Just as you are, they are doing the best they can.

• Practicing patience means relinquishing control. Just as you cannot truly control your life, you cannot control your grief. You can set your intention to embrace your grief and take steps to mourn well. And these practices will certainly serve you well on your journey, but you cannot control the particulars of what life will continue to lay before you.

CARPE DIEM

When you are feeling impatient, silently repeat this
phrase: "My grief is on its own course. It will take its time,
and if I fight it, it will take more of my time."

25.

LET GO OF DESTRUCTIVE MYTHS ABOUT GRIEF AND MOURNING

"People suffer because they are caught in their views. As soon as we release those views, we are free and we don't suffer anymore."
— Thich Nhat Hanh

- As you've grown and developed throughout your life, you have probably witnessed or experienced losses that directly or indirectly affected you. Along the way it's natural for all of us to internalize many of our society's harmful myths about grief and mourning. You may be familiar with some of the following:

  - Don't cry. Tears are a sign of weakness.
  - People need to get over their grief and just put it behind them.
  - Death is a taboo topic. It's something we don't talk about.
  - The more traumatic the death, the more we should try to put it behind us quickly and efficiently.
  - When other people are counting on you, you need to "hurry up and deal with it" and get things back to "normal."

- If you buy into these myths, they will often cause you to put pressure on yourself to heal. They will also bring up new emotions for you to deal with, including guilt or shame about your true thoughts and feelings related to the death of your sweet baby.

- Remind yourself that these myths are not rules to grieve by. In fact, they will take you off course and delay your grief most of the time. Your grief is what it is, and it's unique, not exactly like anyone else's, even the grief of others who have experienced stillbirth. It's normal and necessary.

CARPE DIEM

Which grief myth has been most harmful to your grief journey? Consider the ways in which you can help teach others about these destructive myths.

26.

WEAR A SYMBOL OF MOURNING

"He that conceals his grief finds no remedy for it."
— Turkish Proverb

- In centuries past, mourners identified themselves in some way to communicate that they were torn apart and in the process of grieving after the death of someone loved. Wearing jewelry or wreaths made out of locks of hair that belonged to the person who died were common practices. Black clothing, or mourning clothes, were required to be worn for a period of one year. Sometimes mourners wore black armbands.

- These symbols of mourning accorded a special status to mourners, saying, in effect, "Someone I love has died. Please offer me your respect and condolences."

- Today we no longer identify mourners in these ways, creating the harmful illusion that "everything is back to normal"—even thought it's not and never will be.

- How do you let others know you're still in mourning and still need their support? The best way is to tell them. Talk about the death and its continuing impact on your life. Let your friends and family know you still need reassurance, love, and help.

CARPE DIEM

Make a symbol of mourning part of your everyday dress.
Wear a certain piece of jewelry, such as a black band on your
finger or around your neck. Or you might fill a locket with
a photo or wear a button with a quote or photo on it.

27.

KNOW THERE ARE NO BAD DAYS, ONLY "NECESSARY" DAYS

"It is no use saying, 'We are doing our best.' You have got to succeed in doing what is necessary."

— Winston Churchill

- Many parents talk about having "bad" days more often than not after the death of their child. What they mean is that they have spent a majority of the day crying, feeling extremely sad, or unable to really engage in anything productive. These are days that you likely dread and that make you feel as if you are not progressing toward integrating this loss.

- Yet these "bad" days are actually days when your body and mind have insisted that you mourn. What would happen if you were able to perceive them as "necessary" instead of bad?

- It may be difficult to give yourself permission to just embrace these days. Because they surface without warning, embracing them may seem impossible. If you could plan for them, that would make it easier. Over time your grief will not shanghai you like this. It will not take over your life so thoroughly, from hour to hour, and day to day.

- So often our grief lingers because we are fighting it every step of the way. We are telling ourselves what we "should not" do—we should not still be crying or we should not still be so debilitated—rather than allowing ourselves to cry deeply, without pause.

CARPE DIEM

What does surrendering fully to your grief mean to you? Describe to your partner or to a companion in grief what the moment that you fully surrender and befriend a wave of grief is like.

28.

REACH OUT TO OTHERS WHO TRULY UNDERSTAND YOUR PAIN

"It is not in the going down that we demonstrate resilience, it is in the getting up again."

— Ingrid Poulson

- If at times you feel alone, we want to remind you that you never are. Parents of the two million stillborn babies born each year across the world share the tragic experience of their babies dying before birth. Stillbirths occur more often than SIDS, and more babies die in stillbirth than are diagnosed with Down Syndrome. There are countless other bereaved parents who know and feel the pain enveloping your heart.

- These parents understand that the death a baby before birth is a particularly painful experience. Your experience differs from other parents who have lost a child to miscarriage, though often others may interact with you as though the losses are the same. You carried your baby for at least 20 weeks. You took care of and bonded with your sweet baby for months as she developed inside of you. Your connection to your baby was very real, and you felt a deep sense of love for her even before birth.

- Other parents who have gone through a stillbirth loss will understand better, but still not perfectly. The circumstances around the pregnancy and stillbirth between two mothers or fathers may be very different from one another.

- Reaching out, listening to what has helped other parents survive, embracing their empathy, and hearing their messages of hope will make this journey more tolerable.

CARPE DIEM

When you are ready, look up area support groups or Google online resources focused on helping parents after their baby is stillborn. Find a place where others openly share their stories and can truly empathize with your loss.

29.

KNOW THAT YOU WILL REACH THE OTHER SIDE OF GRIEF

---

*"When you are sorrowful, look again in your heart,
and you shall see that in truth you are weeping
for that which has been your delight."*

— Kahlil Gibran

- When your baby dies, the pain is excruciating. We want you to know that you will find your way to the other side of this pain and grief you are experiencing right now. You will survive this loss, and the pain will not always be this present in your heart.

- Some parents who have lost a baby through stillbirth also struggle with feeling that they don't *want* to survive. Surviving may feel too painful at times. While this feeling is normal and will pass, it is important that you talk with someone when you are feeling this level of hopelessness and despair.

- The way to the other side is through—through the hopelessness, through the pain, through the wilderness of grief. One day in the not-too-distant future, you will feel that there is a purpose in your life and life is worth living again. For now, think of how important you are to your remaining children if you have other children, to your partner, to your own parents, to your siblings, and to your friends.

- As you mourn over time and integrate painful thoughts, feelings, and memories, you may find yourself not simply surviving, but truly thriving. You may come to live with peace, joy, presence, and love in your everyday life. The remainder of your life can be full and satisfying if you choose to experience life rather than merely exist.

CARPE DIEM

If you are feeling that your grief feels unsurvivable, find a way to gain power over it. Draw a picture of it. Find a song that seems to articulate your grief experience more than your own words can. Give your grief a name, a face, or a voice. Expressing your grief in this way may diminish some of the power it has over you today.

30.

BELIEVE IN YOUR CAPACITY TO HEAL

*"The healing of our present woundedness may lie in
recognizing and reclaiming the capacity we have to heal
each other, the enormous power in the simplest of human
relationships: the strength of a touch, the blessing of
forgiveness, the grace of someone else taking you just as
you are and finding in you an unsuspected goodness."*

— Rachel Naomi Remen

• Again we want to remind you, because you cannot be reminded
enough of this: You will survive this.

• In moments when you do not believe you will get through another
moment, another hour, another day...cling to the knowledge that
you will survive. When you feel the depth of your panic or despair
and you are certain that you will never feel joy again…know that you
will survive. When you feel you have no more strength or energy to
face the day...breathe in and out...and remind yourself that you will
survive.

• Part of healing is believing that there is a path to healing and that you
have the capacity within you to heal. Remember, the path to healing is
not the five "stages" of grief. Your path to healing is to find ways that
feel right for you to actively, openly mourn this death. To go deep
into your pain and feel it, trusting that this ultimately will heal it.

• Healing is also about believing that in the moments when you have
nothing more and feel like giving up, others will be there to carry you
through until you muster up enough to stand on your own two feet
again.

CARPE DIEM

How do you believe healing occurs? Consider other tragedies
that you know people have survived and perhaps even gone
on to thrive. Think about stories you've heard on the news
or true stories on the big screen, like *Alive* or *Soul Surfer*.
What gave those people the "capacity to survive"?

31.

MOVE TOWARD YOUR GRIEF,
NOT AWAY FROM IT

*"It is in dialogue with pain that beautiful
things acquire their value."*

— Alain de Botton

- Our society teaches us that emotional pain is to be avoided, not embraced. Others will advocate that it's better to not be in pain and encourage you to move away from your pain. Yet it is only in moving toward our grief that we can be healed.

- Remember, the only way to get to the other side of anything is through it.

- Be suspicious if you find yourself thinking that you're "doing well" since the death. Sometimes doing well means you are not allowing yourself to feel your grief and you are avoiding the pain that is naturally present when we lose someone we love.

- Of course, it is also necessary to dose yourself during grief. Sometimes you will need to distract yourself from the pain. But, in general, you should feel that you are moving toward your grief— toward an understanding and integration of it.

CARPE DIEM

Take note of all of the people in your life who love you and who loved your baby. Pick one or two of them to contact today, and talk about how you feel you loved your baby. Allow them to share their love of this child with you too.

32.

ACKNOWLEDGE THAT YOU AND YOUR CHILD HAD A RELATIONSHIP

"'O'hana' means family. No one gets left behind, and no one is ever forgotten."
— Chris Sanders and Dean DeBlois, *Lilo & Stitch*

- When do you think your relationship with your child began? Some parents who have experienced stillbirth say it was the moment they found out they were pregnant. Others say it was when they began planning the pregnancy. Still others feel it began when they first felt the baby move. Whatever your belief about this relationship's beginning, it's vital to acknowledge that you and your child did share a relationship. While in the womb, the baby was being cared for in many ways. You and your partner were connected to this baby before, during, and after the newborn's birth. You are still connected.

- To remind yourself of how precious this relationship was, take a moment to reflect on the ways that you related to your child in utero. Did you talk to the baby, hold your (or your partner's) belly as if you were holding the baby, rub your pregnant belly, or play music for the child? Did you nurture and nourish the baby? Did you create a space in your life for the child, perhaps a baby room or purchased items that the baby would need to be cleaned and clothed?

- You and your baby had a relationship, albeit not the relationship you hoped and dreamed of. You formed a bond in ways that you perhaps have not even considered until now.

- Understanding that there was love and attachment to your baby is an important part of understanding your grief. When we lose something we love and cherish, our natural response is to grieve. You loved and cherished your baby.

CARPE DIEM

Give yourself permission to think, talk, or write about
how you expressed love to your baby throughout your
pregnancy as well as after the baby's birth.

33.

GIVE ATTENTION TO YOUR MARRIAGE

*"Remember that a successful marriage depends on two things:
(1) finding the right person and (2) being the right person."*

— Unknown

- It's been said that divorce is prevalent when parents lose a child. In our experience, however, this is no more true for you than it is for a couple who has not encountered a loss like yours.

- Your baby's death does not have to be a fatal blow to your marriage. If you loved your partner before the death and intended to stay married forever, there is no reason your marriage cannot continue to succeed. Yes, your marriage may need more open communication and attention in the coming months and years, but it is not doomed to fail.

- When a couple works on their marriage, this means they communicate about all that goes on in life. Marriages need attention every day. The death of your newborn is just one part of your life together. Right now it may be the most painful part. Working on your marriage means talking openly about how this loss is influencing your daily life and how it is changing you. It also means spending time together, both in work and in play. It means figuring out the stressful matters that may be felt, including financial stressors or differences in intimacy needs right now. It means sharing dreams and joys as well as failures and sorrows.

- People may say to you, "At least you have each other." This may not feel like a blessing in moments when you both are so overcome with grief. But in other moments it is wonderful to have a person you can count on, who is present to you and cares about how your day feels.

CARPE DIEM

Look into a marriage retreat or talk to your partner about
meeting with someone who can help you open up about all of
the ways this loss is changing your marital relationship.

34.

EXPECT TO HAVE WHIRLWIND EMOTIONS

"Your intellect may be confused, but your emotions will never lie to you."
— Robert Ebert

- Your loss does not just leave you feeling deeply sad. You may also experience other emotions right now, such as numbness, anger, guilt, fear, worry, regret, confusion, and, for some parents, relief (in situations where the baby was not going to have a good quality of life even if she had survived, for example).

- Sometimes these feelings follow each other within a short period of time. Sometimes they may whirl together simultaneously, leaving you uncertain about what you are feeling. Think of these moments as those when you allow your grief to be present in your life as a chord (many notes all at once) rather than a string of several single notes one after another.

- Embracing the whirlwind and the single emotions is a difficult but necessary part of the journey. You may spend most of your day trying to avoid, prevent, or ignore the painful emotions from surfacing by keeping busy or distracting yourself. Every day, find a brief period of time that you can allow yourself to just feel whatever comes up. Without judging the feelings or yourself as good or bad, right or wrong, just feel. It may also help to put words or pictures to your grief when you make space and invite it to surface.

CARPE DIEM

Have your grief feelings surprised you? Which ones have been the most unexpected for you? Tell your partner or a friend about the surprising feelings and allow him to bear witness to your emotional experience with this loss.

35.

TALK ABOUT GRIEF AND MOURNING

"Grief shared is grief diminished."
—Rabbi Grollman

- Maybe you could teach what you are learning about life, love, and loss to others. Tell your friends and family about the six needs of mourning. Share with them how important it is that mourners have others who companion them in grief rather than "treating" them as if they have an illness to be cured.

- "Healing" your loss and "curing" your loss are two different concepts. Healing is an active emotional and spiritual process in which you seek to be whole again. Curing is a medical term that implies that someone or something outside of you rids you of your grief. Your grief cannot be cured; it will always live inside of you.

- Share your wisdom in the safety of a grief support group that focuses on supporting parents who have experienced a stillbirth. Encourage the group to try to distinguish their grief from their process of mourning. Teach them what you know about this distinction.

- Remember that each person's grief journey is unique. Your grief journey will be influenced by many factors, including the circumstances of your baby's death, your pregnancy experience, as well as the support received in the hospital and beyond. Your experiences and wisdom will not be appreciated by everyone, so remember that it's not personal if someone does not agree with your understanding of grief.

CARPE DIEM

Write your own definition of grief and mourning. Perhaps you can even put a picture or drawing to each word or definition. This will help you to actually see how has your grief is different from your mourning.

36.

BE TOLERANT OF AN IMPERFECT FUNERAL

"There is a kind of beauty in imperfection."
— Conrad Hall

- Many parents who chose to have a funeral or service for their baby have shared that it was not as perfect as they would have liked it to be. They wanted a perfect goodbye for their precious angel.

- For many parents, the death came without warning. Funeral and burial decisions may have been made quickly, while you were still in shock and disbelief. Sometimes some of the decisions may seem wrong or inadequate in hindsight.

- If you harbor any negative feelings about your baby's funeral or memorial service, know this: You and everyone else did the best you could at the time. You cannot alter what has already been, but you can talk about what you experienced. You can share your thoughts about what you would have done differently. You can talk about why this experience was challenging and what could have made it easier for you.

- It's never too late to hold another memorial service. A tree planting or small gathering on the anniversary of the child's death could be a forum for sharing memories and expressing emotions. Ask a clergyperson or someone you know who's a good public speaker to help plan and lead the ceremony. This time, include the elements that you may not have been able to before. Play certain songs, buy a type of flower that's meaningful, serve a particular food, and share your story if you can put words to it now.

CARPE DIEM

When words are inadequate, create ceremony. Which elements of ceremony would you like to include in your child's service? Music that expresses something about your grief or about your precious child? Candles held by or lit by those who join you? Pictures of your baby? Make a list of the elements that you want to be sure to include if you hold another ceremony in honor of your baby.

37.

ACKNOWLEDGE THE MULTITUDE OF LOSSES

"The death of a child is the single most traumatic event in medicine. To lose a child is to lose a piece of yourself."

— Dr. Burton Grebin

- After your baby died, you may have also experienced the loss of a sense of security. Many parents describe that they feel betrayed (this was not supposed to happen, after all) and unsafe (it was unexpected, and for some parents, the cause may still be unknown). You may no longer trust others and the unfolding of life in the same way you once did.

- One of the most difficult losses for grieving parents is the loss of hopes and dreams for the future. You have not had the opportunity to get to know your child and witness her personality. The loss of seeing her smile, tickling her, soothing her when she cried, and rocking her to sleep are important to openly mourn.

- When your baby died, his future also died with him. Your dreams of helping him learn to sit up on his own, take his first steps, utter his first words, use a sippy cup, learn to potty train, enter preschool, get ready for his first school pictures, and the many years of growth beyond these joyous childhood milestones are irrevocably shattered.

- Allowing yourself to acknowledge the many layers of loss that your newborn's death has brought to your life is vital. To move forward in your grief journey, outwardly acknowledging the multitude of losses that you are encountering is an important part of your movement.

CARPE DIEM

Name your many losses out loud to someone who is able to just sit and listen without trying to "make it better." Describe openly and honestly the opportunities you will not have with your baby that you were looking forward to. Put words to the future experiences or events that you'll mourn as a result of your baby's early death.

38.

WATCH FOR WARNING SIGNALS

*"The most common way people give up their
power is by thinking they don't have any."*
– Alice Walker

- Understandably, when you are going through such a difficult time, it's easy to fall back on self-destructive behaviors as a way to get through. You may feel the pain of your baby's absence and want to fill the space with something that will help you escape this pain.

- What are your signals that you are not doing well?
    - Do you sleep too much or, perhaps you are not sleeping well at all?
    - Are you using drugs or alcohol to self-treat your pain?
    - Are you isolating yourself?
    - Are you overeating or restricting your eating?
    - Do you feel restless and anxious most of the time?

- Try to be honest with yourself, as these are all signals to you that you need to ask for help. If others approach you about any behaviors that concern them, please listen to them.

- Seeing a grief counselor is probably a good idea if you had a history of substance abuse, depression, or anxiety prior to your baby's death.

- If thoughts of hurting yourself or taking your own life have crossed your mind, even passively, talk to someone about your depression so that you can expand your thoughts about life and living.

CARPE DIEM

Acknowledging to ourselves that we have a problem may come
only after we have started on a downward spiral emotionally or
behaviorally. If someone suggests that you need help outside of
your family and friendship circle, consider yourself lucky to be so
well-loved and ask them to help you find someone to talk with.

39.

IDENTIFY A PERSON YOU CAN COUNT ON

*"Friendship isn't about whom you have known the longest
... It's about who came, and never left your side."*

– Unknown

- You may have many people who you are absolutely sure care about you. But not all of these caring others are going to be good companions to you in grief.

- Someone who companions you in grief is able to bear witness by inviting you to touch your emotional pain and allowing your tears to flow without trying to stop you. She is willing to listen without giving you advice or telling you how you should feel. She is able to allow you to take this at your own pace, instead of pulling you forward because she wants you to "get over" your grief sooner than your natural pace.

- Though we would like to assume that everyone who loves us will be able to walk with us in this way, it's important to know that even very compassionate people sometimes find it hard to be present to others in grief.

- If any of your closest friends seem to have abandoned you, don't assume that you can't count on them. They probably need you to take the lead by inviting them to talk with you about your newborn's death. Invite this friend or family member to lunch, be candid about your feelings, give them the companioning philosophy, and teach them directly how they can help.

CARPE DIEM

Watch a movie about true friendship. Notice which characteristics are important to you in a true friend. Which qualities or actions tell you that someone really cares and reassures you that you can count on that person?

40.

SET BOUNDARIES

"When you respect your own 'NO!' then others will, too."

— Rae Shagalov

- The experience you went through with your baby was one of the most emotionally draining that a couple can share. You had to say hello and goodbye to your precious baby within a short period of time. Within that window of time, great sorrow was part of your first face-to-face encounter with your son or daughter.

- Especially if this is soon after the stillbirth, you may find that your body lacks the energy to participate in activities you used to find pleasant. You may not even feel a desire to connect with others in the same ways that you have in the recent past. Your body, mind, and soul need time to recuperate.

- It's OK to say no when you are asked to attend an event, join a group, or spend time with friends. Saying no can be done politely but firmly. Let people know that you can't participate right now, but you appreciate that they asked. If you communicate better in writing, write a note, email, or text to the person who invited you and explain that you appreciate that he reached out, but the time is not right now.

- Isolating yourself from friends or social groups over a long period can result in the loss of your support network and loneliness in your grief. If it begins to feel as if your grief is resulting in your missing out on life's most joyful celebrations—birthdays, weddings, performances by your children—this is signaling that you may be pulling inward too often. Finding a balance between being alone and being with others while you are grieving is vital.

CARPE DIEM

It can be difficult to set healthy boundaries for yourself. Take some time to consider what boundaries are absolutely necessary right now for you given that your energy level may be more limited. Take the things that you can off your plate to make room for your mind and body to begin the healing process.

41.

PREPARE TO ANSWER
UNCOMFORTABLE QUESTIONS

*"Don't duck the most difficult problems. That just ensures
that the hardest part will be left when you are most tired.
Get the big one done—it's downhill from then on."*

—Norman Vincent Peale

- What were once happy, even exciting questions to answer are now
riddled with pain and can trigger high emotions. Which questions do
you dread being asked? How will you answer them?

> *Weren't you pregnant?*
> *Did you just have a baby?*
> *How did your delivery go?*
> *What did you name the baby?*
> *Where is your baby?*
> *Why did they make you deliver the baby?*
> *How many children do you have now?*

- For some parents, leaving out the name of the child who died may
seem disloyal or like a lack of acknowledging the child's birth. Saying
your son or daughter's name and then having to explain the death often
transforms what would have been a very casual conversation. It is OK to
include your baby's name, however, even if it changes the conversation.
Here are a few ideas:

> Yes, the delivery was a difficult. My baby died before she was delivered.
> We named the baby Alyssa before she died.
> I have two children here on earth, and one baby angel waiting in heaven.
> I have three children. Emily is five, Tommy is three,
> and my youngest baby, Sara, died at birth.

- Most bereaved parents report that answering these questions gets easier
and more natural over time. The more prepared you are to answer, the
easier these uncomfortable moments will be.

CARPE DIEM

What would be the most difficult question someone
could ask you about this loss? Take a moment to decide
how you would answer it if you are asked.

42.

CARRY A LINKING OBJECT

"We cannot change our memories, but we can change their meaning and the power they have over us."
— David Seamands

- As a parent you may find comfort in physical objects that belonged to or are associated with your baby. Linking objects will help you remember your baby and honor the time that you had with your child in utero and in the hospital. These objects may be an important part of your healing process.

- Know that it is not unusual to save objects like the ultrasound picture, baby and mothers' ID bracelets, a special blanket, baby booties or cap, the outfit the child was going to wear home from the hospital, a pacifier, a small lock of hair, the baby's handprints or footprints, the certificate of stillbirth, or a birthstone.

- Never think that being attached to these objects is morbid or wrong. If someone tells you that you are crazy for wearing your ID bracelet with your son's name on it or not washing the blanket your baby was wrapped in when you held him in the hospital, try not to listen. You're not crazy; you're simply holding on to what you have left of your precious infant.

- Never hurry into disposing of your baby's belongings. You may want to leave personal items untouched in the nursery for months or even more than a year if there is no need for the room to be changed. This is OK as long as the objects or belongings offer comfort and don't inhibit healing. You will know they are inhibiting healing if you find that after many months you haven't experienced any emotional movement toward embracing the reality that your baby has died and your relationship with your baby is one of presence, not of memory.

CARPE DIEM

When and only when you're ready, ask a friend or family member to help you sort through your baby's room and the belongings you've saved. Fill a memory box with significant objects and mementos. Find a place in your home to hold these precious items so that you can return to see and hold them anytime you desire.

43.

SHARE YOUR STORY

*"Live your life from your heart. Share from your heart.
And your story will touch and heal people's souls."*
— Melody Beattie

- Your baby's stillbirth is an important part of you and your life story. So far it's a story that spans from the moment you were thinking about conceiving this child to right now in this moment. It is your story and it is a story that, when given a voice, will become a more integrated part of you rather than something that "happened to you."

- Acknowledging your baby died is a painful, ongoing process that you will work on in doses over time. A vital part of dosing yourself is going to involve telling the story over and over again. Each time you tell the story, it becomes a little more real and more an integral part of you.

- Your "story" is the circumstance surrounding your daughter or son's death, your view of the relationship you had with your baby during pregnancy, your time with the baby after birth, your memories of the baby's physical body, aspects of what you dreamed of your baby's life being like, as well as memories of the baby developing in utero, the delivery, and the sinking moment you learned that your baby had no heartbeat.

- Find the person or people who are able to really listen and will allow you to tell the story, over and over again with as much detail as you need, without jumping in, advising you, or judging how your story unfolded.

CARPE DIEM

Try to tell the story through a series of songs. Find four or
five songs that reflect what you experienced through the
conception, pregnancy, and death of your baby. Make a CD
and give a copy to your family, friends, and other children.

44.

USE LANGUAGE THAT EMPOWERS YOU

"Words are the keys to the heart."
— Chinese proverb

- The language we choose to use affects how we think and feel about ourselves, our lives, and about the death of someone loved.

- Passive language such as "our baby is gone" can make us feel like victims. We feel that life and loss happen to us rather than happen in spite of us. Using stronger, active language like "our baby died before we could save him" can help us regain some sense of personal power in the face of death.

- If your baby died, for example, from a complication due to trauma to the child's mother (a care accident, domestic abuse, or an intentional action by someone to harm the baby), you may feel more empowered to say that he was "killed" rather than he "died."

- Although our culture encourages euphemisms, avoid them. Saying that your baby "passed away" or was "lost" may seem gentler, but these words don't truly describe the emotional jolt of your baby's death. Practice saying the words that more accurately describe your experience, such as "My baby died suddenly" or "My child is dead."

- Similarly, work to find words to describe how you are really feeling about your baby's death. When someone asks, "How are you?", it's OK to be brief but honest. Perhaps you can honestly say, "I've been feeling really (sad, angry, lonely, lost, or heartbroken)." Or "This week was really hard for me because..."

CARPE DIEM

Are there certain words that people use when talking about your baby's death that bother you? The next time you hear them, let the speaker know why his words are painful to you and offer to share other words that may be more comforting if he is open to hearing them.

45.

USE YOUR BABY'S NAME

"Every baby born into the world is a finer one than the last."
— Charles Dickens

- Talking about your baby by name is difficult for some parents after stillbirth. Some parents may not have chosen a name, because it was not something that they were invited to do or they weren't sure what name would have been best. If you did name your baby, know that it's good for you to refer to him by name. It is your way of validating his existence.

- Be aware that friends or family may be afraid to use the baby's name in your presence. When others do not use your baby's name, you may wonder if they have forgotten about him or don't care enough to call him by name. In reality, they may just fear it will bring up painful thoughts or feelings. What most may not understand is that those painful thoughts and feelings are ever-present.

- When you're talking to others and you use the child's name, this makes everyone aware that it is OK or even preferable to you.

- If you feel you can be direct, ask your friends and family to use your child's name too. You may love to hear that special name and to know that others think of the child too!

- It will be helpful as you mourn to acknowledge the significance of this loss in your life by purposefully talking about your child. When talking to your partner, a friend, your mother, or your other child, you might say, "I was thinking about Ally the other day because..." or "I wonder if Ally knows that we miss her..." or "All I want to be doing right now is carrying Ally...my arms feel so empty right now."

CARPE DIEM

Flip through a baby name book. Look up the name of your child. Reflect on the meaning of the name as it relates to what your dreams and hopes were for your daughter or son.

46.

TALK TO YOUR BABY

*"If the others heard me talking out loud they would think
that I am crazy. But since I am not, I do not care."*

— Ernest Hemingway

- If your baby were sitting with you, in your arms, and you could tell her how you are doing, what would you say? If you were able to tell her what you miss about her, what would you share? If you were able to say anything, what words would you express to her?

- Talking out loud to someone we know has died can feel strange at first. We aren't sure where they are or if they can hear us. For some parents, it's simply enough to know that it's possible that the child can hear them.

- Talking is a way of connecting. Even if the person we are trying to connect to isn't responding, a connection can still occur. It's just coming from one direction. In fact, this is the way many connections are made in parent-child relationships at various times throughout childhood because children do not always reciprocate connection (such as when they are sick, irritable, or their adolescent hormones are raging).

- Because your baby is not physically present any longer, it may make it easier to talk out loud to her if you can look at her photos or hold something that belonged to her, such as a blanket. If you feel it would be easier, visit the cemetery to sit and have a conversation near her grave. Or when you pass his nursery, talk silently to your child when you are on your way to bed each night. Or go in and read a bedtime story out loud for her. If you have a photo, make it part of your daily routine to say good morning to that photo on your nightstand.

CARPE DIEM

If you haven't already, put a photo of your baby in your wallet
or purse. Make it a habit to look at the photo and tell her what is
going on in your life that day. Tell her you how big your love is.

47.

REDEFINE "BIRTHDAYS"

---

*"Fly free and happy beyond birthdays and across forever,
and we'll meet now and then when we wish, in the
midst of the one celebration that never can end."*

— Richard Bach

- Your baby died before or on the day she was born into this world. You and your family experienced a tremendous loss on what should have been your child's birthday. From that day forward, birthdays may take on an entirely different meaning for you and your family.

- This may not be a day of celebration for you, but it will be a day of memory and meaning. It's OK to hold some type of gathering on this day or to spend the day with just your immediate family. It's OK to light a candle, buy a card, or even give gifts to the people you love in memory of the love you had for your precious infant. Perhaps, at some point in your grief journey, you will feel comfort knowing that you have not forgotten how old your child would be and perhaps even wonder if your child has been growing in another place that you may refer to as heaven.

- Some parents want to differentiate the baby's birthday from the baby's date of death, so they choose to honor her birthday on her due date or on a different special day of their choosing. You are the one who is able to decide which days are meaningful to you.

CARPE DIEM

If you have the energy, plan something with your family so that
you spend your baby's birthday doing something that you all
feel good about—perhaps volunteering, doing something none
of you have done before, or buying something for a child who
is the same age as your baby would have been this year.

48.

BE AWARE OF "GRIEF OVERLOAD"

*"Unexpressed emotions will never die. They are buried
alive and will come forth later in uglier ways."*
— Sigmund Freud

- Unfortunately, sometimes we experience more than one loss in a short period of time.

- Have you experienced any other losses—the death of a friend, a parent, or a grandparent—in the past few months or even the past year? If you have, you may not only be feeling the grief around this tragic death of your precious child but also the grief of other losses.

- You may also have recently experienced other types of losses that are stressful and invite the need to mourn. Have you experienced any major changes in your life—such as a career change, a divorce in your family, a diagnosis of a chronic or life-threatening illness—that you may also be grieving alongside the death of your baby?

- If multiple losses have shaken your life, you may be at risk for what can be called "grief overload." Your ability to cope with change may be stretched beyond its limits. You may think of nothing but death if you are grieving multiple deaths. You may feel torn, grieving one death this minute and another death the next. You may feel like you are going crazy because you feel engulfed by death and grief.

- Be assured, you are not going crazy. You are, however, in need of special care. The challenge here is finding ways to cope with all the stress of everyday life, while also creating the space you need to grieve.

CARPE DIEM

If you're in grief overload right now, sit down and make a list of
five things you can do right now to help reduce some of your
stress. Make it a point to take action on these five things today!

49.

IF YOU ARE ANGRY, FIND APPROPRIATE WAYS TO EXPRESS YOUR ANGER

"Holding on to anger is like grasping a hot coal with the intent of throwing it at someone else; you are the one who gets burned."

— Buddha

- If your baby's death was sudden and unexpected, it's normal to feel intensely angry. Anger is especially common in cases when parents feel that someone is at fault for the death. You may obsess over your feelings of rage and hate the person you feel is responsible—a doctor, yourself, or someone who caused an incident that led to your baby's death. In cases of accidental death, you may direct your anger at God or at fate, such as being in the wrong place at the wrong time.

- Logically or illogically, you may feel angry at others around you, sometimes for no reason other than that your baby died and their baby did not. You may be angry at the other mothers who are giving birth at the hospital, at pregnant women you see, at your spouse for his response to the death, at your doctor for his non-emotional response to your baby's death or for not listening to your concerns during pregnancy, or at your mother or best friend because she has not suffered as you have. Some parents have also shared that they have felt angry with the baby for dying, feeling the baby abandoned them when all they wanted to do was to love and care for her.

- Like all of your feelings, anger is not wrong. It simply is. What you do with your anger can be wrong, however. If you are angry and isolate yourself in anger, you may slide into chronic depression. Express anger in healthy ways. Never harm yourself or someone else in an attempt to squelch your rage. This will only hurt you in the end.

CARPE DIEM

Today, vent your anger through physical activity. Run instead of walk. Go for a hike. Throw rocks across a lake or in a field. Punch a boxing bag. Go to a batting cage and hit the ball hard, over and over again.

50.

LEAVE HURTFUL ADVICE BEHIND

"Nobody can give you wiser advice than yourself."
— Marcus Tullius Cicero

- Sometimes well-meaning but misinformed family members or friends will say something that is hurtful, unknowingly wounding you with their words:

    - I know how you feel.
    - Your baby is in a better place.
    - It's time to move past this and get on with your life.
    - Keep your chin up.
    - This is probably a blessing in disguise.
    - At least you can still have other children.
    - Think of all you have to be thankful for.
    - Now you have an angel in heaven.
    - It will be OK.
    - You will feel better in time.
    - You're strong. You will get over this.

- Please do not take these misguided words of advice to heart. Leave them in the moment or the space in which they were said. Let them dissolve into the air instead of taking them in and carrying them with you. Try not to let your anger over people's seeming insensitivity get the best of you. Such clichés are often offered because people don't know what else to say. You know, for example, that there is no "better place" for your newborn than in the arms of her parents. You know that these comments dismiss your pain and diminish the reality that this is a unique and significant loss, but others may not be aware.

CARPE DIEM

Take some time today to make a list of the helpful and loving things
that people are saying to you. It's easy to focus on what is being
said that hurts; those are much more memorable moments. Turn
your attention instead toward the words and deeds directed your
way that offer a sense of love, support, and comfort to you.

51.

FIND WAYS TO MOVE THROUGH ANY DOUBT AND GUILT

*"I was always fraught with guilt, and it's such
a waste of an emotion. It keeps you out of
the moment of being where you are."*
— Kyra Sedgwick

- When a baby is stillborn, some newly bereaved parents feel guilty that they didn't do everything perfectly during the pregnancy. Some parents feel that they weren't protective enough or nurturing enough to their body to help the baby survive. Some experience guilt that they didn't even know the baby was dying. Still others regret that they were not as alert as they wanted to be during the delivery so that they could hold their baby right away. Do you run things over and over again in your mind to try to identify what could have happened?

- Do you believe you were responsible for your child's conception? Or was some greater power responsible for that miracle? Is it possible that perhaps the baby's stillbirth was equally in the hands of a greater power? If you are feeling responsible, talk to a counselor about any feelings of doubt, guilt, regret, or remorse.

- Talk openly with your partner, a supportive friend, or a counselor about lingering feelings. Feeding these feelings by thinking about them over and over again and continuing to punish yourself is not going to help you, your partner, or your other children. Expressing them may diminish the power they have over you right now.

- Rationally or irrationally, some parents blame their partners for some aspect of the death. If feelings of blame reside in you, talk compassionately to your partner with the help of a counselor. Remember that his or her heart is also broken.

CARPE DIEM

Write a letter to yourself or to your newborn. Start with something like this, "I need to share what I think may have happened..." Get any feelings of guilt, resentment, or regret out and onto paper. Then find someone who will simply listen to these feelings you have been carrying inside.

52.

TAKE CARE OF YOU!

"Beauty is how you feel inside, and it reflects in your eyes."
— Sophia Loren

- Sometimes when we are in mourning we feel weighted down, dull, or muted. You may wonder if what you are feeling on the inside is somehow visible to others on the outside. It's not always bad to look bad because it allows others to see how you feel on the inside. If you find yourself feeling unattractive or dull, know that it's natural for your self-esteem to be affected by your grief.

- You may not be bothering with your appearance right now because you have low energy or it doesn't seem as important as it once did. You might be telling yourself, "It doesn't matter if I do my hair or get dressed to go out today. I just lost my baby. That's what matters." You are right. The grief in your heart needs your attention right now.

- Yet, part of good self-care and healing is practicing to love and value life again, including your physical life. Take a look in the mirror and compassionately reacquaint yourself with you. This doesn't mean you should be over-focused on your appearance or your physique. It means that your broken heart isn't the only facet of your being that needs your attention right now.

- Your emotional state can and will change when you change your physical state. Smile for 30 seconds right now (a full 30 seconds). You can feel something change in you physically. Now, frown for 30 seconds, and you'll feel your emotional state change again. Smile one more time (to end with a smile!), and experience the remarkable ability you have to alter your emotional state with a simple shift of your physical self.

CARPE DIEM

You can do anything with this time. There is no pressure to engage in an activity or to spend money. This is just 10 minutes of "me" time that you gift to yourself each day. Why? Because you deserve to be taken care of!

53.

MAKE SLEEP A PRIORITY

"Sleep is the best meditation."
— the Dalai Lama

- During the first few months after your baby's death, you may notice that it's harder to fall asleep or that your tend to wake up during the night. Changes in your sleep pattern are normal and reflect your special needs right now.

- The longer you go without adequate sleep, the more your sleep deprivation will influence your mood, tolerance of others, and energy level. You may feel like you make up for poor sleep during the week by sleeping in on the weekends, but this is not as beneficial for your body as getting a consistent number of hours of sleep nightly.

- How many hours of sleep do you need to feel really rested? Find a sleep-inducing technique that is effective for you and that you are willing to use nightly, such as:
  - creating a relaxing reading ritual in bed.
  - taking a warm bath just before bed.
  - lighting a scented candle or incense that induce sleep, such as lavender.
  - listening to a theta wave CD that promotes sleep.
  - drinking Sleepytime tea before bed.

CARPE DIEM

If you or someone in your family is having trouble sleeping, create a sleep basket that anyone in the family can use. Fill it with items and ideas that will help promote sleep. Some things you might include: warm milk recipes, chamomile, dream catchers, Sleepytime tea, a lavender sachet or scented candle, bath salts, and a list of ideas for clearing the mind and relaxing the body.

54.

HONOR WHAT YOUR BODY NEEDS

"Your body is precious. It is your vehicle for
awakening. Treat it with care."
— Buddha

- If you are the mother, your body has been through a great deal. It has been carrying this precious child for months. It was physically preparing for you to give birth, then nourish and nurture a newborn. Your mind was mentally and emotionally preparing for this same experience.

- For many expectant parents, the birthing process is exhausting, but that exhaustion subsides because your body and mind know they need to kick into full gear to care for a newborn. Your body and mind have been through the same process only to find that there is no place to direct those natural instincts to nourish and nurture.

- You may not know what to do with your nurturing instincts. Right now your body needs care and attention, so perhaps that is where these instincts can be placed. Eating regularly, getting into a sleep cycle, taking daily baths, using lotion to soften your skin, and soothing any aches and pains that arise are all important right now. Self-care is necessary for mourners, yet it's something many of us push aside.

- You may not trust your body and second-guess the signals it gives you now. After all, you may have thought your baby was developing and growing just as he should. Your body was not signaling to you that anything was wrong. Try to work on trusting what your body is telling you right now. When you are fatigued, rest. During grief, when we do not listen to our bodies, they will find a way to get our attention with a cold or an illness that will force us to slow down and rest.

CARPE DIEM

Identify which part of your physical needs you are neglecting most right now. Sleep? Nutrition? Relaxation? Exercise? Move that need to the top of your priority list this week. Make a conscious effort to make sure that need is met every day over the next seven days.

55.

CREATE A PERSONAL SANCTUARY JUST FOR YOU

"Sanctuary, on a personal level, is where we perform the job of taking care of our soul."
— Christopher Forrest McDowell

- When grief, loss, and the need to mourn enter your life, you need a dedicated safe space to call your own. You need a private territory where you can explore self-development and spiritual practices as well as read insightful books, meditate, journal, or simply contemplate the universe.

- A personal sanctuary may be "your" seat or pew in your place of worship. It could be a garden in a park or a hiking path or a bench on the grounds of a retreat center. Sanctuaries are usually sanctified in some way to invite in and help you connect to the Divine. You can create a sacred space in your home by smudging the room or adorning it with items or furniture that help your mind focus on your spiritual self. You can say a special prayer or chant to designate that it is set apart from other rooms in your home as a sacred space.

- Use earthy paint colors, find a cozy chair, and consider installing a tabletop fountain in the space. You may want to be able to play gentle music that brings sounds into the room that remind you of spirit or the Divine (the ocean, gentle drops of rain, drumming, or flutes). Or maybe you want this space to be dedicated to silence. As author Thomas Moore wisely noted, "Silence allows many sounds to reach awareness that otherwise would be unheard."

CARPE DIEM

Consider what you want to feel when you are in your sanctuary—harmony, for example. Find colors for the walls, the sound that you would like to vibrate through this space while you are present, and photos that resonate a meaningful message to you. Surround yourself with that message through colors, sounds, sights, and smells.

56.

LET GO OF TENSION WITH A SIGH

"Breathe. Let go. And remind yourself that this very moment is the only one you know you have for sure."
— Oprah Winfrey

- You can release tension and stress through your breath. When you take a deep breath in through your nose, filling your belly (not your chest), you can imagine that your breath is like a sponge soaking up tiny particles of tension that sit within you. When you are ready, release all of that tension you've gathered through an audible, outward sigh.

- Sighing is an easy way to release or let go of something you are holding onto. We are, in a way, accepting that there is something present in us and that we have the capacity to move it from the inside of us out.

- For some, sighing is like a form of prayer more powerful than words. In the Bible, Romans 8 describes that when there are not words for our prayer, the spirits intervene and pray for us. Their prayer comes in the forms of sighs, sighs deeper than anything that can be expressed in words.

- Allow your body to sigh. Sigh deeply. Sigh whenever you are in a space where you feel comfortable sighing. With each sigh you are acknowledging through a conscious action that you have the ability to control your breath, but you are not in total control of your life.

- Think of each sigh as your prayer for your precious baby. You are not letting go of your baby or your love for your baby as you sigh. You are letting go of the hold that your pain seems to have on you now that your baby has died.

CARPE DIEM

Right now, take a deep breath in and hold your breath for a count of five. Then with an open mouth (jaw dropped), sigh, pushing that breath outward as loudly and deeply as you can. Do this slowly five times in a row. Do you feel as if you have emptied something from yourself?

57.

TURN OFF THE NEGATIVITY

"Dwelling on the negative simply contributes to its power."
— Shirley MacLaine

- When we experience a major loss or feel overwhelmed with stress in our lives, our natural instinct is to want to shut things down—shut people out, shut noises off, and shut out the chaos going on around us. In order to survive, our mind and body instinctually want to shut doors instead of opening them.

- Right now there is no need to surround yourself with unneeded noise or demanding people who take away energy rather than provide comfort or support. Negativity and stress is all around us; it may be very helpful to find ways to set good boundaries around yourself so that negative information does not keep coming at you.

- You might consider turning on the television less often or taking a hiatus from the daily news or newspaper. Violent videogames, movies with depressing storylines, and the dystopian books that are so popular right now may be things you want to eliminate for at least a few weeks. If there are people in your life who seem to always complain or focus on what is wrong rather than what is good in the world, minimize your contact with them for a bit. Going to places that are busy and chaotic, such as the mall or restaurants, may also be something you want to take a break from. Try it and see if your days feel less heavy when negative or depressing information is not coming at you.

- Spend time with people who have positive and warm energy. Spend more time in places where you know others are going to be sending you messages of hope, life, and light.

CARPE DIEM

Make a list of the sources of negativity right now. Are there clear limits you can set without feeling guilty for giving yourself a break from these people, places, or experiences?

58.

HOLD SOMEONE

*"Love consists in this, that two solitudes
protect and touch and greet each other."*

— Rainer Maria Rilke

- Were you able to hold your baby after he died? This may be one of your most precious memories of your child.

- Love and sweetness naturally flows from us when we hold a newborn baby in our arms. Do you remember your loving instincts surfacing when you held your precious baby? Newborn babies are a reminder of the simplicity of life and love.

- When your baby was born, it was supposed to be a moment in which life and light entered the room. Instead, your baby was inside of you during his life, and your baby's birth was what we talk about as the other end of life—an ending, a very sad ending, here on earth.

- Because your baby is not here to hold, find someone you can hold— another newborn baby, one of your other children, a niece or nephew, your partner. Embrace and hold that person in your arms. Notice how it makes you feel. Find other ways to make this same feeling part of your everyday life.

CARPE DIEM

How long have you gone without being touched? Touching is
such an important human need. Sometimes there is not someone
around whom we can touch or be touched by. If you need to,
schedule a massage or spa time that involves a treatment in
which your feet or hands or back are touched and nurtured.

59.

REMEMBER, ROCKS CRUMBLE WITH TOO MUCH WEIGHT

*"I want to weep, she thought. I want to be comforted. I'm
so tired of being strong. I want to be foolish and frightened
for once. Just for a small while, that's all...a day...an hour."*
— George R.R. Martin

- In the face of loss, the common responses is to try to buck up and stoically be a rock-solid source of support for others around you who are also grieving. If you are the person in your family who is taking on this role as the "rock," be aware that it will be difficult to sustain this.

- Fathers are especially vulnerable to being the "rock" after a loss. Others may even encourage you to do this by saying, "Be strong for them" or "Your family is counting on you to carry them through this." Try not to let these statements misguide you into believing it's best to ignore your own grief or trauma. In a flight emergency, whose oxygen do you need to strap on first in order to help your child or partner who is sitting next to you? Your own! Making sure you are taking care of your grief first, in doses, is essential to supporting your family through this.

- It's natural to want to keep some solid ground while your family is going through this difficult time, but you can do this in ways other than emotional stoicism. Solid ground can be found by bringing structure into your home, being consistent with how you respond when your child or partner is actively mourning, following through on what you say, reminding your family that you are always someone they can count on, and making sure you are accessible when your family needs you.

CARPE DIEM

Redefine what it means to be "strong" during this grief journey. Take a minute to write down your definition and the actions that embody that definition. Make sure that at least once a week you do something (talking with someone, expressing emotions, or physically releasing your grief) that actively helps you express the grief you are carrying.

60.

CREATE YOUR OWN PLACE TO KEEN OR WAIL

"That's the thing about pain...it demands to be felt."
— John Green

- You may find yourself experiencing periods where you cry so deeply that your body wails or moans as an expression of pain. This is called *keening*, and it is a natural, outward expression of the deep, raw pain that you may feel in your core. Allowing yourself to keen means giving yourself permission to release the deep sorrow that entered your life when your baby died.

- Some cultures have places that invite mourners to wail and keen in order to reach, release, and honor their sorrow. The Wailing Wall in Jerusalem is the holiest place on earth for Jews. It is the remains of the great Jewish temple of Jerusalem. It is thought that when praying at the Wailing Wall, you are in the presence of the divine. Jews from all countries and tourists of other religious backgrounds come to pray at the wall into "the ear of God." Prayers written on little pieces of paper call *tzetzels* are placed into the cracks of the wall. Those who cannot travel to Jerusalem can send prayers to be read and placed in the cracks of the wall.

- You can create your own wailing wall or place to mark your grief. It could be a wall in your garden in which you tuck notes about your grief, a book in which you slip grief notes between pages, a jar you fill with thoughts written on small pieces of paper, or a bulletin board where you pin notes, quotes, or memories. Or maybe you know of a wall in your community that you can adopt as your wailing wall—a place where you can go to cry out in pain and anguish.

CARPE DIEM

Wailing and keening are forms of mourning. Find a way that you can allow yourself to "wail" today. It will help you reach your deep inner wound. In order to heal, this wound needs to be touched, and the pain within it released outwardly.

61.

FIND THE WORDS IN MUSIC

*"Give sorrow words; the grief that does not speak knits
up the o'er-wrought heart and bids it break."*

— William Shakespeare

- When we cannot find the words to express what we are feeling or thinking, it's amazing how music and lyrics have a way of saying what we need to, but cannot.

- Have you heard a song that reminds you of how you feel about your relationship with your baby or about your baby's death? Is there a song that you listened to while you were pregnant that speaks to you? Is there a message that you want your baby to know (or others to know) that you were not able to give him the way you had planned because he died too soon?

- Find a song or songs that allow you to express the thoughts and feelings that are so jumbled inside of you right now. Make a playlist, and when you want to consciously set aside time and space to mourn, listen to your playlist and let your emotions surface.

CARPE DIEM

Have you ever happened upon a song that triggered deep emotion in you? Turning off the radio to avoid these "griefbursts" seems easier than feeling the pain they trigger. But these songs can be helpful in your grief journey. We encourage you to create a time each day or week and listen to them somewhere you can allow your grief to surface and flow from the inside of you out.

62.

TELL SOMEONE YOU LOVE HER

"Silent gratitude isn't much use to anyone."
— Gladys Browyn Stern

- Your baby's death has you very aware of how precious and important love is in this world. Love makes people smile, and the presence of love can help us through the most trying of times.

- Sometimes we love people but forget to put our feelings into words or actions. We don't say "I love you" as often as we could. We may believe that they already know, so there is no need to say it. We might assume they can feel it or see it through our actions, so it doesn't need to be spoken. Gifting these three words to another person—"I love you"—is a gentle reminder to them that whether they feel it or not, whether you've shown it or not, it's true.

- When they are spoken out loud to someone with whom we have a strong connection—our child, our spouse, our parents, our lifelong friend—these three simple words take on a deep spiritual meaning. Yet we sometimes fail to see the significance of saying these words until it's too late.

- Who in your life would you like to hear more "I love yous" from? Who do you know in your mind loves you but doesn't say the words? Even if you are not receiving the words from them, make it a priority to say these words to the people in your life. Let them hear it come from you so there is no doubt, no assumption, just acknowledgment that love exists.

CARPE DIEM

Call someone you love right now and give her the
lasting gift of telling her you love her.

63.

SING OR PLAY A LULLABY

"Luminaries play to a darkened sky. Each
life is a star in the night's lullaby."

— Jill Hanna

- Sometimes it feels good to connect with your baby in the same ways you would have if he were physically here. You would be talking to him, asking him questions that he could not answer anyway, holding him, rocking him, and perhaps even singing to him.

- Lullabies are a way that many parents connect with their newborn babies and send messages of love, warmth, and harmony.

- Were there lullabies that you grew up with? Lullabies that you sang to or played for your baby while in utero?

- Although your baby is not physically present, as a way to reconnect with your precious child, play the song, sing the words, or learn to play it on an instrument.

- If you want to make it a part of your daily routine, consider beginning or ending your day with a lullaby dedication to your baby, communicating that your son or daughter has made an imprint on your heart and soul.

CARPE DIEM

Ask your mom or dad if there were any songs that they sang to or played for you as a child. You had a special connection to your child, so you would know best which lullabies you would have liked to have played to help him sleep, calm down, or transition during naptime. Make a playlist of these songs and play them whenever you desire.

64.

KNOW THAT IT'S NORMAL TO FEEL THE PRESENCE OF YOUR BABY

"To be loved means to be recognized as existing."
— Thich Nhat Hanh

- It is important to acknowledge right here and right now that your baby was real. She existed. We know, and you know from your experience of the baby, that your baby was very much alive. Your baby could not have died if she was not first alive. This is not something that everyone in your life may understand. In fact, their words and actions may communicate the opposite message to you.

- Sometimes after a child dies, no matter what the age or circumstances, parents express feeling the presence of their child. They are going about some everyday activity and suddenly feel their child is there with them. Or they have a vivid dream in which their child shows them what heaven is like. Or something unusual happens in their day and the parents perceive it as a sign from their child.

- These kinds of experiences can seem very real and often are reassuring. If you've felt your child's presence, you're not crazy. Who is to say what's real and what's imagined when it comes to grief? What matters is your love for your child and your continued feelings of connection to her. Perhaps that connection is what you are feeling.

- If you've felt the presence of your baby since he died, tell someone about it. Be sure to choose someone who is open-minded. Often such experiences are welcomed (but not always understood) by others. Regardless, these stories are often a wonderful reassurance to us all that death is not the end.

CARPE DIEM

If you've felt your baby's presence, write down your story
and share it with someone close to you. If you do not know
who to share it with right now, tuck the story away with your
private papers so that you can find it another day, or perhaps
someone else will find it one day and be comforted by it.

65.

ACKNOWLEDGE WHEN YOU
ARE FEELING "LOST"

"Not all those who wander are lost."
— J.R.R. Tolkien, *The Fellowship of the Ring*

- Death is not what you were preparing for. You were preparing for life! After the birth, your days and nights were no longer going to be your own. Daily life was going to be filled with tasks like diaper changing, breast- or bottle-feeding, laundry, bathing, rocking, and soothing.

- Both your body and mind were preparing for this experience. Sleepless nights throughout pregnancy are common for both mothers and fathers and help parents prepare for the sleep deprivation, constant demands, and vigilance that they will need to care for a newborn baby.

- You may experience many moments of feeling lost and unsure what you are supposed to do now. You may at times feel you are supposed to be doing something—anything—motherly (or fatherly), yet unsure where to put this energy. Your mind may lead you to engage in some caretaking behaviors even though your baby is not here, such as cleaning the baby's room or folding and refolding the baby's clothes. And you may actually take care of your baby after death, perhaps by placing a grave blanket on the place where your baby is buried in the winter or placing flowers near her ashes.

- Acknowledge out loud to your partner and to yourself when you are feeling "lost." It will help you to stop and take a moment to dose yourself with the painful reality that your baby is not here for you to take care of. Express your pain (moan, sigh, cry, talk) as you engage in a task or action that you feel is meaningful to you. These moments of feeling lost are a natural part of this grief journey. Be compassionate with yourself as you wander through the first weeks after the death.

CARPE DIEM

Create a caregiving list for yourself. This list is a way to remind you of the many ways that you are still caretaking right now. Though you are not taking care of your baby, you are taking care of yourself, your partner, and perhaps your other children as you begin to move through your grief.

66.

ACCESS GOOD GRIEF SUPPORT ONLINE

"Grief knits two hearts in closer bonds than happiness ever can; and common sufferings are far stronger links than common joys."

—Alphonse de Lamartine

- Social support in all forms provides connection, a sense of community, a ritual in our day, and, for some, a needed sense of anonymity. Talking with other parents who have also experienced stillbirth can give you a glimpse into what life after stillbirth can be. You may hear stories from other parents that give you a sense of hope and reassurance. You may also encounter other bereaved parents and think, "That is not where I want to be a year from now." While some stories may seem discouraging at first glance, recognize that knowing where you *don't* want to be can be just as helpful as knowing where you *do* want to be.

- Social connections online come in many different forms—discussion groups, memorial pages, picture boards, book clubs, blogs—so finding the one that feels right to you is important. Perhaps even starting your own online outreach through a blog will be one of the ways that you discover a sense of meaning or purpose after this death.

- Learn more about resources that are available to you through the International Stillbirth Alliance as well as other agencies that provide support during and after stillbirth, including Now I Lay Me Down To Sleep, *Still Standing* magazine, and www.stillbirthday.com.

CARPE DIEM

Design a memorial page or a Pinterest page for your baby. Invite friends and family to post their thoughts and supportive words on it. Allow yourself to open it and read other's supportive words when you need to be reassured that you are not alone.

67.

ALLOW FOR UNFINISHED BUSINESS

"Courage is being afraid and going on the journey anyhow."
—John Wayne

• Death often brings about feelings of unfinished business. Time was something you had very little of with your sweet baby. There were so many things you didn't get to say, perhaps things you said that you wish you hadn't during your pregnancy, and things that you were unable to do because of the sudden and early nature of your child's death.

• Is there something you wanted to say to your baby but didn't have enough time or weren't given the privacy to say? Is there something that happened during your pregnancy or during the birth that you feel regretful about? Is there an action you wish you could take right now, if you had the chance to be with your baby just one more hour or one more day?

• Allow yourself to think about and feel the emotions related to all that feels "unfinished." Your "if onlys" may never fully be resolved in your mind and heart, but if you permit yourself to put them outside of yourself (to give voice to them, to mourn them), you will be able to reconcile even those that you are not able to finish.

CARPE DIEM

Perhaps you have some task that you have been putting off, a goal that is incomplete because you have not had time to do it. Finish that task and take note of how it feels to complete something that felt undone.

68.

SIMPLIFY

*"Life is really simple, but we insist
on making it complicated."*

— Confucius

- There is no better time than now to take stock of what's really important in your life. Once you do this, you may find that it is easy to discard what is weighing you down or not serving you.

- As a parent who is grieving, it's easy to become overwhelmed by all of the tasks, demands, and commitments you have—taking care of your other children, keeping your marriage healthy, meeting demands at work, keeping your home up, fulfilling your obligations to committees you're on, helping others who need you. If you can rid yourself of some of those extraneous burdens, you'll have more time for your family and for healing.

- What is overburdening you right now? Have your name taken off junk-mail lists. Hire someone to clean your dirty house. Stop attending any optional meetings you don't look forward to or are unnecessary right now. Ask someone to help you with meals or your other children. Let your friends know that you will need to take a hiatus from PTA, carpool, or your neighborhood book club if you are part of these. Ask a friend to help you with running errands, getting groceries, paying bills, etc.

- Often your family and friends would like to help but don't know how or what to do. Make a list of the things that need to get done in a day then choose at least three of these that you can ask someone else to help with for the next month or so.

CARPE DIEM

Have a family meeting and take stock of your family activities calendar. Ask everyone present which activities they truly want to continue and which they would be happier without. Make cuts where appropriate. Maybe you can even fill in some of the extra time you all have with a little vacation.

69.

PREPARE YOURSELF FOR
THE HOLIDAYS

*"For many people, holidays are not voyages of
discovery, but a ritual of reassurance."*
— Philip Andrew

- Perhaps you envisioned what the holidays were going to be like with a newborn baby. Because your newborn is not physically here, you won't share the holidays with him in the same way that you imagined. You may feel particularly sad and vulnerable during family gatherings like Thanksgiving, Christmas, Hanukkah, and Easter.

- It is common in our society for people to overextend themselves during the holidays. Try not to put pressure on yourself to do all of the shopping, baking, entertaining, and mailing of holiday cards if you are not up for it.

- Sometimes participating in traditional holiday rituals can feel comforting after a death, and sometimes it does not. Continue them only if they feel good to you; consider creating new traditions if that feels better.

- If you are able to find a way to make remembering your baby part of your holiday ritual, this may help you feel the holidays are more fulfilling. For example, you could decorate a small tabletop tree each year at Christmas in honor of your baby. On the tree hang ornaments, photos, special mementoes such as rattles, or other little toys. Or purchase a special ornament or make a special dish (angel food cake) that can be a way for your family, without words, to know that you are all thinking of your precious baby who is not here to celebrate this special day with you.

CARPE DIEM

What's the next major holiday? Make a plan right now and let those
you usually spend the day with know what you are planning.

70.

DREAM

*"The best thing about dreams is that fleeting moment,
when you are between asleep and awake, when you don't
know the difference between reality and fantasy, when
for just that one moment you feel with your entire soul
that the dream is reality, and it really happened."*

— Unknown

- After a stillbirth, many parents share that they dream about their baby. Dreaming about your baby can bring about feelings of relief, contentment, even joy. Though many parents have described feeling that waves of grief hit them when they wake, because once again they feel the loss of their child, they long to see their child in another dream.

- Try not to be afraid to sleep and dream about your baby. Dreaming of your baby is your body and mind's way of trying to connect with and process what has happened. You have a deep internal desire to see your baby. Your brain helps you reach that desire. Perhaps in the dream you will have the opportunity to touch or hold your baby longer than you had the chance to in real life or say something to your baby that you did not get to say.

- Your interpretation of your dream is likely the closest to what is true. Rather than letting someone interpret or prescribe meaning to it for you, write down what you felt in the dream, recall details of the emotions you felt, and seek to know the dream message that first comes to mind from your heart and soul.

CARPE DIEM

Start to keep a dream journal. Track your dreams for a few weeks and see if you can find any comfort in your dream world. Perhaps you can learn more about what you need right now or what you are struggling with most. If you are seeing a counselor for grief support, you can take this information in with you. It may provide some additional insight.

71.

DEMONSTRATE YOUR FAITH

*"Faith is taking the first step even when
you don't see the whole staircase."*
— Martin Luther King, Jr.

- Above all, mourning is a spiritual journey of the heart and soul. The death of your newborn gives rise to the most profound spiritual yearnings and chaos. You may find that this loss has invited you to examine your beliefs about death and develop an understanding of where God or your higher power fits within your suffering.

- If you have faith or a spiritual side, express it in ways that seem congruent with who you are and what you are going through right now.

- Attending church or your place of worship, reading religious texts, and praying are a few conventional ways to express spirituality. If meditating, hiking, or spending time alone in nature resonate more with your spiritual needs, make time each week for those activities.

- For many grieving parents, having faith means holding the belief that they will one day see their baby again. This belief alone, whether the reconnection will be in heaven, through reincarnation, or in a less-defined afterlife, makes getting through the days more bearable for some parents.

- Do you believe you will be reunited with your baby one day? If you do, allow yourself to revel in this belief. Close your eyes and envision your concept of heaven. See your child seeing you. See her welcoming you, reaching out to you. Retreat to this hope-filled image when you are feeling disconnected, filled with sorrow, or discouraged.

CARPE DIEM

Find a quote or two on faith that resonate with you. Reflect on
what it is about the quote that speaks to you. How have you
demonstrated your faith at this point in your grief journey?

72.

KNOW THAT YOU ARE
A GOOD PARENT

"A mother understands what a child does not say."
— Jewish proverb

- If you find that you are questioning yourself, you are not alone. Stillbirth often generates so much self-doubt and self-admonishment that parents become their own worst critics.

- Doubts about whether or not you were a good parent and did the right things for your baby through the pregnancy or birthing process are normal. Some parents ask themselves questions about whether they made the right choice about autopsy or feel guilty that their baby was in the morgue and not in their arms. Others wonder if they held their baby long enough, tight enough, lovingly enough before they had to leave the hospital. Still others wonder if perhaps the death is a sign that they would not have been good parents to this baby.

- Some of these doubts are spurred by what others ignorantly say. Some parents feel questioned or blamed. Has anyone asked you, "Couldn't you tell that the baby wasn't OK?" Other doubts arise because parents are trying to find a way to control what was completely out of their control.

- Most people who have not experienced stillbirth are unaware of the process and what you had to go through as parents. They ask questions that seem absurd like, "Why did you decide to deliver the baby?", as if the baby somehow disappeared inside of you after the doctors told you that she died.

CARPE DIEM

When self-doubt enters your mind, rather than feeding these doubts, take a moment to shift your thinking. Rather than interrogating yourself about what went wrong, reflect on the actions you took that demonstrated that you were indeed a good parent to your baby.

73.

GROUND YOUR THOUGHTS
WITH A TOUCHSTONE

"Dreams are the touchstones of our characters."
— Henry David Thoreau

• A touchstone can be a very useful tool during your grief journey. Touchstones can be used to help you set an intention or to bring a behavior into consciousness, a behavior that you want to emulate in your everyday life.

• Let's say that you want to "be kind" no matter how others respond to your loss. When you are deciding how to react in a difficult situation, such as when someone says something inappropriate or dismisses the significance of your loss, you might be tempted to explode in anger. When you are focused on your touchstone, you pause before the anger erupts. You consider your "be kind" mantra and instead decide that an angry outburst would be counterproductive and hurtful to you as much as it would be hurtful to the other.

• We recommend that you literally carry a stone in your pocket to remind yourself of an intention or touchstone you would like to emulate. Whenever you're feeling your grief or struggling with a thought or feeling, put your hand in your pocket and hold the stone. Remind yourself that you want your response to come from a place of "kindness," if that is your intention. The stone's smooth surface will help center you and return you to your place of conscious living.

CARPE DIEM

Go to a specialty shop to purchase a rock with a meaningful
word or phrase on it that touches your heart, such as
"patience," "gratitude," "hope," or "connection." Or make
a touchstone using a rock from your own backyard.

74.

COMMUNICATE WITH YOUR PARTNER ABOUT YOUR SEX LIFE

"I wonder if this is how people always get close: they heal each other's wounds; they repair the broken skin."
— Lauren Oliver

- Parents in grief often struggle with how and when to continue their sex lives. This struggle is often present because one partner may be consumed with their grief or feel so completely misunderstood that sex is the last thing on his or her mind.

- Beyond the waiting period that is recommended by doctors after a woman gives birth, couples struggle around how and when to reengage sexually after stillbirth. The meaning of sex and the act of sex can take on a whole new meaning, especially to mothers who have given birth to a stillborn baby. Acknowledge that sex has changed for you as a couple. Now, finding a way to reinitiate that important part of your relationship is vital.

- If one partner wants to start having sex again and the other does not, it's important to talk openly about this reality. It is also critical to talk about why it is not wanted or why the timing is not right, so that assumptions are not being made by either person. Insisting or guilting your partner into anything he or she is not ready for will only breed resentment that will come out in other ways in the relationship. If it becomes too difficult to talk about without help, seek a trusted counselor who can facilitate this sometimes-difficult conversation.

- Eventually, most couples settle back into their normal sexual pattern. If you don't see this happening in your marriage or are unhappy with your sex life, it may help to work with a marriage counselor who is aware of the special needs of couples who have lost an infant.

CARPE DIEM

Talking about sex can be difficult or embarrassing for some couples. If you are having a hard time talking about it, perhaps find some other ways of communicating about your sexual wants and needs. Try writing each other notes or reading a book on marital intimacy together.

75.

MANAGE YOUR FEARS ABOUT FUTURE PREGNANCIES

"Life is available only in the present. That is why we should walk in such a way that every step can bring us to the here and the now."

— Thich Nhat Hanh

- Going through a stillbirth can bring up many fears for you as parents, especially if and when you begin to contemplate having another baby. Naturally, you will wonder if stillbirth could happen again. You may also wonder if you are going to be able to love another baby the way that you would have loved the baby who died.

- Others may tell you that having another baby right away, if you can, is best. Though it's misguided, this may be their way of trying to help you put your grief aside rather than integrating it. The truth is that only you know when and if you will be ready to try to become pregnant again.

- Sometimes people think that having a live baby in our arms will make everything all better. But it will not take away your awareness of who is missing. The new baby's birth may be joyous but also bittersweet.

- Sometimes others will want to reassure you that your next pregnancy "will go OK," which may not feel very reassuring at all. It's natural for you to wonder if it will go OK next time.

- There is no right time to consider future pregnancies. What is most important is that you have been actively working through your grief and that your body is physically ready to carry another child full-term. When you are ready, consider reaching out to support programs designed to help you and your family through your next pregnancy.

CARPE DIEM

Take some time to list all of the fears, questions, and thoughts that have gone through your mind about having another baby. Have your partner do the same. Talk about your fears with one another but also talk about your desire to create another life together and what that means to both of you right now.

76.

BELIEVE IN THE POWER
OF YOUR STORY

*"Memory is a way of holding on to the things you love,
the things you are, the things you never want to lose."*
— from *The Wonder Years*

- Integrating your baby's death is a painful, ongoing task that you accomplish in doses, over time. A vital part of healing grief is often "telling your story," not once but many times as others bear witness to your experience. When the death was the result of a traumatic or violent experience, the shock of the death may delay your need to talk about it for several months.

- Once you are ready to talk about the death, you may feel compelled to think through and talk about details related to "how" (the circumstances) this usually joy-filled experience ended with your baby dying. This is normal and necessary. If your mind returns to the moment of the death often, this is natural. This is your mind's effort to fathom that which is unfathomable.

- What if you don't want to talk about it? It's OK to respect this feeling for weeks and months following the loss, but soon you'll want (and need) to start talking about it. Keeping your thoughts and feelings about the death inside you only makes them more powerful. Trust that you will "tell your story" when you are ready.

- Over time, the story of your sweet child's death will likely evolve from one dominated by the death to one dominated by loving memories of your child. This is a natural progression and a sign that you are healing.

CARPE DIEM

Discuss your story with someone else who loved your sweet baby. This person may also be struggling with questions or confusion regarding the circumstances of the death. Bear witness to this person's story and allow her to bear witness to yours.

77.

CREATE AN ONLINE MEMORIAL

"The heart that truly loves never forgets."
— Proverb

- After your child died, you may have wondered how anyone would ever know him. Perhaps only your immediate family was given the chance to see the baby. If you held a memorial or funeral, this may have been a space where you were able to share your love of your child with those who attended.

- There may be other people in your life who were unable to attend the memorial or funeral ceremony that you would like to share your experience with. You may want to make your baby real to other people who may not fully understand that although your baby was stillborn, he was very much a real person.

- Take some time to create a virtual memorial (on Facebook or some other online forum like the World of Remembrance) for your baby, then invite friends from across the country to see the page and write comments to support you in your grief. You can post photos, poems, and quotes as well as information about stillbirth grief to help others fully understand what you are going through right now.

- This is a wonderful way to acknowledge the precious love you felt for your baby, allow others to know how deeply you miss him, and access support that you may not have otherwise received because you are not in close proximity to some of your friends or family.

CARPE DIEM

What would you like others to know about your baby? You can provide as much or as little information as you like on a virtual memorial. Create a virtual space that you feel represents your precious child.

78.

PUBLISH YOUR WORDS

*"Be yourself. Above all, let who you are, what you are,
what you believe, shine through every sentence you write."*
— John Jakes

- Sometimes friends or family will publish a memorial poem in the newspaper, place a memorial posting on Facebook, write up one for a school newsletter or a bulletin given out at their place of worship, or create a memorial website as a way to honor someone who has died and bear witness to their grief.

- Seeing your words on paper or on the screen, knowing that others are going to see and bear witness to them, may feel comforting to you.

- When you are ready to share your words with more people, take some time to write a message and consider where you would like to have it publicized.

- You can write a message, create a poem, or find a verse that speaks to you. Messages honoring someone loved often appear on the anniversary of the death or another special anniversary. For you it may be the date of conception or the date the baby was supposed to be delivered that you would like to acknowledge by publishing something.

CARPE DIEM

Call your local newspaper or a community magazine to ask if they publish memorials. Find out what the process is and when you need to submit your message for their next publication release.

79.

PLAN A CEREMONY

"Everything is ceremony in the wild garden of childhood."
— Pablo Neruda

- We have been told that stillbirth is one of those life experiences that is difficult to express in words. So, when words are inadequate, have ceremony.

- Ceremony can be healing because it helps us embrace the reality that someone we loved died. It gives us space to recall and share parts of our story. It is a forum for giving and receiving needed support. It is a process that facilitates your movement, your transcendence, from a newly bereaved parent to a parent who is integrating a painful loss.

- Even after the funeral, you can participate in or hold a ceremony. Months or even a year after the death, holding a ceremony can be a very meaningful recognition that your child is not gone but instead lives on in some way. Ongoing rituals such as those we hold for other tragedies (like the World Trade Center deaths) help you continue to both remember and integrate the loss you've experienced into your head, heart, and soul.

- Ceremonies do not have to be extravagant. They can include a small circle of your friends or just your immediate family or a community of parents who have also had a baby die. Candle lighting, tree planting, drumming, or gatherings where you create a memorial piece (like a scrapbook or art piece) can all be forms of ceremony. Your ceremony may also include an affirmation of your faith or spiritual values. In many bodies of faith there are remembering practices or remembering prayers that can also be incorporated into your ceremony.

CARPE DIEM

Hold a candle-lighting ceremony. Invite a small group of friends. Form a circle around the center candle, with each person holding her own small candle. Have each person light her memory candle and share a memory of the pregnancy or a hope for your family. At the end, play a song or read a poem or prayer in memory of your precious baby.

80.

WRITE A LETTER TO YOUR HIGHER POWER

"Babies are bits of stardust, blown from the hand of God."
— Barretto

- Sometimes expressing our thoughts and feelings on paper (in a letter, card, journal, or notebook) helps us to understand them better. When we can remove them from inside of our minds and actually see them in front of us, we can begin to take a different view. Sometimes, free-flowing writing can reveal a great deal about where we are struggling the most.

- If you were to write out your thoughts and feelings to your "higher power," to whom would you address it to and what would you say? Take a moment to write a brief letter now. Express how you feel in this moment. Consider the following prompts:

  - *Right now, my relationship with you is...*
  - *Right now, when I think about my life I believe...*
  - *Right now, my journey through grief feels ...*
  - *Right now, my hopes for the future are ...*

- You might also find it helpful to write notes of gratitude to those people who were or continue to be supportive of you at this time, including hospital staff, friends, family, neighbors, your doctors, and the funeral director.

CARPE DIEM

Take a moment to reflect on how your higher power fits into your everyday life. How do you connect with that which you refer to as your higher power—through prayer, attending church, reading scripture, meditation, yoga, hiking in nature, stargazing etc.? Whatever ways you feel you reach your higher power, take 15 minutes today and spend time contemplating something bigger than yourself.

81.

DON'T BE CAUGHT OFF-GUARD BY GRIEFBURSTS

*"To expect the unexpected shows a
thoroughly modern intellect."*
— Oscar Wilde

- Heightened periods of sadness often overwhelm us when we are in the midst of grief.

- These bursts of sadness, which sometimes feel uncontrollable, seem to come of out nowhere. When they catch you off-guard, especially if you are unaware that they are normal and natural, they can be frightening and painful. But if you expect them as a natural part of your day or week, they may not be quite so overwhelming.

- Even long after the death (a year or two or more), something as simple as a sound, a smell, or phrase can bring on a griefburst.

- Allow yourself to experience griefbursts without shame or self-judgment, no matter where and when they occur. Even if you or those around you don't understand what brings one to the surface, it's there and it is asking to be released. Most of the time, it's only uncomfortable for others because they don't know what to do to stop it. If only they knew that the thing to do is to welcome it, these moments would be much easier for everyone. If you feel more comfortable, retreat to somewhere private when these strong feelings surface.

CARPE DIEM

If you can recall your most recent griefburst, take a moment to write about it in a journal or an email. Identify what triggered the emotion (an object? event? song?). Make note of how you feel now about your expressiveness during that griefburst. If you are ashamed of how it unfolded—how you sounded, how you looked—take a moment and imagine that you were watching someone else behave the same way. What might you have said to him to assure him that it was not only natural but a necessary part of his grief journey?

82.

UNDERSTAND THE CONCEPT
OF RECONCILIATION

*"We can never obtain peace in the outer world
until we make peace with ourselves."*

— the Dalai Lama

- What many well-intentioned family members and friends may not understand is that words like "recovery" and "acceptance" imply that your grief is an illness that must be cured. It also assumes an eventual return to the way things were before the stillbirth. Neither of these are true. You are not ill. Your heart is broken and you are torn apart by this loss. You are not the same person today as you were before your baby died. You have been changed by this experience in big and small ways.

- This does not mean you will live in misery. Remember, when you allow yourself to actively mourn, you not only heal, but you transform as you move through to the other side of your grief. Your life can potentially be deeper and more meaningful even after the death of your precious child.

- When you have reconciled your grief, the sharp pangs of sorrow soften, the constant painful memories subside. A renewed interest in the future begins to overtake the natural obsession with the past and the death. You experience more happy than sad in your days. You begin to set new goals and begin to work toward them. You bond with other people and develop close relationships with others again, less fearful of losing them. Life is experienced again.

CARPE DIEM

Explore your understanding of reconciling your grief. What will your life look like once you have reconciled your grief? What will be in your life that is not present now? What will you feel that you do not feel now? What will you want that you do not want now?

83.

THINK ABOUT WHAT COMES NEXT

"All that we are is the result of what we have thought."
— Buddha

- While you should not set a particular time and course for your healing, it may help you to give thought to other life goals that you would like to reach over the coming months. When we are grieving we are often focused on what happened or how we are going to make it through today. We can quickly lose sight of what comes next and what kind of future we want to create for ourselves or our family.

- Your goals do not have to be enormous. Even simple goals like traveling to a place that you've always wanted to experience, learning to do something you've always been fearful to try, or reading a book that you would enjoy can help you find hope.

- Take a few moments to write a list of short-term goals, goals that you can see yourself doing over the next two months. Perhaps some of the goals could have to do with mourning activities, like making a memory book or taking a yoga class that centers on energetically moving your grief through a series of poses.

- At the same time, write out a few long-term goals about which, a year from now, you would like to be able to say, "I did that!" Reflect on the goals you had as a child or something you dreamed of after college. Be both realistic and compassionate with yourself as you consider what is feasible or what feels right rather than goals that will only add stress to your days.

- Read through your list each day, just to remind yourself of the direction you want to move. Place a copy of your list in a location where you will be able to see it and be reminded that you are giving attention to what comes next.

CARPE DIEM

Transform your list of goals from words into pictures. Draw, use magazines, find photos online if you need to. What do you actually see in your future? Create a visual reminder of what comes next.

84.

MOVE YOUR GRIEF TO GRATITUDE WITH YOGA

"You can clutch the past so tightly to your chest that it leaves your arms too full to embrace the present."

— Jan Glidwell

- Yoga is a three-thousand-year-old tradition that originated in India. The primary goal in yoga is to achieve integration between mind, body, and spirit, creating a "wholeness" or "oneness" in your entire being.

- All yoga postures involve what are called *pranayamas*, or breathing purifications, that enhance inner tranquility. How you breathe during each movement influences the flow of your energy as you transition from pose to pose. Yoga encourages you to breathe deeply to bring oxygen to your cells and exhale slowly to rid the body of toxins. Long, slow, deep breaths can help center you and remind you to be present and one with your body.

- Some yoga studios offer workshops that incorporate body work that is focused on integrating any unhealed energies often associated with grief (shame, rejection, anger, abandonment). Standing balancing poses and back-bending poses that stimulate the thymus gland and begin to open up the heart and chest are often incorporated into this work. Poses include supported fish, camel, and bow, for example.

- Because your body is unique, yoga should be individualized. Yoga, which means union or wholeness, is a science and an art based on time-tested techniques. It is probably best learned with a teacher who can help you focus on alignment in postures and finding the flow of postures that best meets your needs. If you are new to yoga, you will want to start with a class for beginners and later perhaps explore other types of intermediate and advanced practices.

CARPE DIEM

Create an action plan to sign up to take an introduction to yoga class. Get online right now and Google "yoga studios" to find locations near you. If you are more advanced, find a class that will allow you to continue to expand your yoga practice beyond where you are.

85.

CLIMB TO NEW HEIGHTS

"Climb the mountains and get their good tidings. Nature's peace will flow into you as sunshine flows into trees. The winds will blow their own freshness into you, and the storms their energy, while cares will drop off like autumn leaves."

— John Muir

- There are days when you will long to be physically closer to your child. When they come, where could you go that would literally feel "closer"? For some parents, being on top of a mountain after a hike, a boulder after rock climbing, or a peak after a winding drive brings a feeling of closeness.

- Going to higher ground, for many parents, gives them the sense that they are closer to heaven.

- Nature surrounds you as you move upward. You can reflect on a multitude of sights and sounds. Time in the mountains invites you to befriend the beauty of nature and allows you to experience tranquility as well as restore your physical, emotional, and spiritual self.

- Being able to "peak" (make it to the top of) a gorgeous mountain affirms your physical, emotional, and spiritual strength. At the summit the views are breathtaking, and you can celebrate and have gratitude for being alive.

- Take time to climb to new heights and experience this: You have made it to the top of the world, surrounded by the power of Mother Nature. You are enveloped by the sights and sounds but also by the stillness and solitude. You feel so close to God and your soul is calmed amid the beauty. Take a moment to close your eyes and remember your last moment with your baby. Remember—your child is watching over you and cheering you on!

CARPE DIEM

Get your calendar right now. Plan a trip to climb or drive up a mountain near you and allow yourself to be encapsulated in the beauty and power of Mother Nature.

86.

BRING IN MORE LIGHT

*"I will love the light for it shows me the way, yet I will
endure the darkness because it shows me the stars."*

— Og Mandino

- Light is illuminating. It helps us see our way. It represents hope. It is the sign of a new day. Darkness can be just the opposite. It obstructs our vision and sometimes makes us feel afraid and hopeless. But even small amounts of light can help dispel those fears.

- Ask any child who is afraid of the dark and he will tell you that what helps is to bring light into his room. If you are feeling like you are in the darkness (and many new bereaved parents do feel this), make a conscious effort to bring more light into your space.

- Find creative and unique ways to light up the darkness you are feeling in your life space right now. Even when it's soft, light can be comforting, like a beacon in the night.

  - Buy nightlights for your hallways and other rooms.
  - Put candles in different rooms and light them when you are spending time in those areas.
  - Repaint walls with a lighter color to brighten up your space.
  - Keep your blinds and curtains open.
  - Purchase a lava lamp or unique lamp to be placed somewhere in your home.
  - Find a neon sign and find a way to add this to your decor.

CARPE DIEM

Take an afternoon and go nightlight shopping. You can find a
variety of nightlights, from stained glass to ceramic to seashells
to pressed dried flowers. If you have other children, pick out
a nightlight that you feel each of them would like. Give the
nightlights to them with a wish for peaceful nights. If you do
not have other children, pick one out for your master bedroom
and perhaps one to give as a gift in memory of your child.

87.

RELAX WITH AROMATHERAPY

*"Behave so the aroma of your actions may enhance
the general sweetness of the atmosphere."*
— Henry David Thoreau

- For centuries people have understood that certain smells or aromas can induce certain emotional and behavioral responses. Aromatherapy is the contemporary term for this age-old practice.

- How does aromatherapy work? It's believed that the inhalation of certain aromas stimulates and signals the limbic system in the brain. The limbic system controls emotions and learned memories. This signaling can result in the release of a chemical in the brain that brings about relaxation, calmness or, depending on the oil, alertness and stimulation in the body and brain.

- A few comforting smells that often induce calming memories include freshly cut grass, pine, chicken soup, and popcorn. Lavender induces relaxation for some. Rosewood and bergamot together lift the spirit. Peppermint has been said to invigorate the body. Chamomile has been associated with better or more restful sleep.

- Essential oils or other aromatic plant compounds can be found at your local drugstore, organic food market, or bath and body shop. Many of these can be added to bath water, burned as incense, or dabbed lightly on pulse points.

CARPE DIEM

Visit a local bath and body shop and choose one or two essential oils or scented candles that smell good to you. Try lighting the candle while you are doing something that involves just being present, for example taking a bath, having coffee, flipping through a magazine, sitting in contemplation, or listening to soft music. Keep the essential oils with you so that you can dab them on your wrist throughout the day or take a breath in when you need to pause and relax.

88.

TAKE IN THE SUN

"The sun illuminates only the eye of the man but shines into the eye and the heart of the child."

— Ralph Waldo Emerson

- The sun is a powerful symbol of life and renewal. It exudes warmth and light, which are both helpful to those who feel they are in the darkness of grief.

- When was the last time you watched the sun rise? Do you remember being touched by its beauty and power?

- Plan an early morning breakfast or walk in a location where you can see the sun rise. Hike to the top of a hill or a nearby lake where you can sit on a blanket and experience the dawn of a new day. Have coffee on a patio where you can see the sun rise. Sometimes you may have trouble sleeping and may be up early anyway. Invite a friend to share the rising sun with you.

- Watching the day begin like this could be emotional for you. The sunrise signifies newness, which is what you expected to experience with the birth of your baby. It's OK if emotion is part of your sunrise experience. Continue to watch as you let your emotions pour out.

CARPE DIEM

Invite a friend on an early morning drive. Choose a fitting destination for watching the sun rise. Pack a brunch—hot coffee and fresh fruit, perhaps. Take a photograph of your sunrise so that you can be reminded of it on other days when you are not so fortunate to witness it in person.

89.

CONTEMPLATE LIFE
THROUGH THE ARTS

"Art washes away from the soul the dust of everyday life."
— Pablo Picasso

- The visual arts have a way of making us see the world anew. In art we can find new perspectives, new ways of looking at ourselves, our relationships, and our surroundings. Art comes in so many forms. What kind of art do you tend to enjoy?

- After someone we love dies, we tend to spend more time in contemplation, and sometimes visual arts invite us to do just that. Perhaps a visit to an art gallery, a museum, a sculpture garden, a photography exhibit, or a botanical garden would be refreshing for you.

- If you have found a piece of art that reminds you of your child or your parent-child connection, frame it and place it in a place that feels right to you.

- If you are creative, why not try to create a work of art yourself? Attend a watercolor or calligraphy class. Making pottery is something almost everyone enjoys. It's tactile and messy and whimsical. Cocktails-and-canvas classes are a way for families to commune and engage their artistic side together.

- Creating artwork is a great way for all of you to express your thoughts and feelings about the love, grief, and ongoing connection between you and your baby, even after death.

CARPE DIEM

Buy some paints, brushes, and a canvas. With your whole family or by yourself, paint the feelings you are filled with right now about your baby. They may be feelings of peace, sorrow, anger, regret—or a mixture of many emotions. Don't worry about your artistic abilities; just let your hand and imagination take the lead.

90.

CONTEMPLATE THE UNIVERSE

"There is only one corner of the universe you can be certain of improving, and that's your own self."

— Aldous Huxley

- Stargazing can be a relaxing, renewing activity that even our children might want to participate in with us. Taking in the darkness, the solitude, the constellations, and the depth of the space around the earth can foster frank conversations about the circle of existence, the meaning of life, and the experience of death.

- Do you have a telescope? If so, get it out and refresh your memory on how to use it. If you don't have one, gazing at the night sky with the naked eye can be equally as awe-inspiring.

- Invite someone (a friend, your other children, someone who knows more about the universe than you) to take a drive in the country where city lights won't obscure the starlight or to take a night hike to the top of a small mountain. Bring a blanket so that you can lie on your backs and stargaze in comfort.

- If you are unable to find the right place because you live in a city, make a plan to visit your local planetarium and contemplate what is much larger than yourself. What does that mean to you? Reflect on how the death of your baby fits into this larger perspective of life and the universe we are a small part of.

CARPE DIEM

Look it up online or visit your local library to gather information about when the next interesting cosmic event will happen (such as a meteor shower, a blue moon, or an eclipse). Invite someone to accompany you to a good viewing spot and stay up to watch something that may only occur once in your lifetime.

91.

ALLOW LOVE IN

"I have found the paradox that if you love until it hurts, there can be no more hurt, only more love."

— Mother Teresa

- For months you gave love and care to your baby. In small ways, perhaps you also received love from your baby—when he would kick or move, for example. But when a newborn takes that first breath and cries out to fill his lungs with air, then nuzzles comfortably in our arms, most parents are flooded with that reception of love that they have waited nine months to experience.

- When a baby is stillborn, parents do not have this experience with their baby, and in fact, the guilt, confusion, and sadness they feel may begin to block their desire or willingness to receive others' love. If you are unsure about why you are feeling guarded or closed off more than normal, this may be part of the reason. As you move through your grief, you will begin to open up your heart again. But in the early days of grief you are so torn apart you will naturally try to protect your wounded heart.

- To help reacquaint yourself with receiving, take a few minutes for this exercise: Select a person you know well and feel at ease with. Take him to coffee or invite him over. As you sit together, have your friend share something that he has noticed you have done well or something he appreciates about you. To be receptive, simply listen and allow the words to enter without making an excuse or explanation about why it's not true. Notice where you are uncomfortable or find yourself wanting to discount what the friend says. Breathe deeply for a minute as you continue to open yourself to this gift of receiving. Sit with it until you can fully accept this verbal gift. Show your gratitude nonverbally by saying thank you with a bow or nod. Now balance it with a giving statement by carrying out the same process for your friend.

CARPE DIEM

At the end of the day, take note about what you took into your well of reception from others. Did you accept a hug or a gift or kind words without pushing them away or minimizing their value?

92.

EXPRESS YOUR CHILDLIKE SELF

*"There is no point in being grown up if
you can't be childish sometimes."*
— Doctor Who

- Sometimes you will need a reprieve from the overwhelming sadness and the glaring reality that your sweet baby died. Wouldn't it be amazing to be able to go back to a time when you were a kid, when you were innocent and carefree, before loss touched your heart?

- It is the nature of children to live for the moment and appreciate what is right in front of them. They know how to live and enjoy "right now." All of us would benefit from inviting a little more childlike energy into our lives.

- The beauty of it is, you can do this! All you need to do is create the time and decide the what and where and with whom you'd like to express your childlike self.

- How long has it been since you rode your bike without having an agenda of exercise, chewed bubblegum, fed the ducks in a pond, laid on your back in the grass, went wading in a stream, ran through a sprinkler, shuffled barefoot across freshly mown grass, had a snowball fight, or built a sandcastle?

- Give yourself permission to do something childlike, such as blow bubbles, jump rope, learn to yo-yo, visit a toy store, fly a kite, or climb a tree.

- If you have older children, invite them to join you for your play date. If the baby who died was your only child, find someone else to join you. You could invite a friend's child, your partner, or a friend who can take her adult hat off and let inhibitions go.

CARPE DIEM

Right now, leave your inhibitions behind. What are one or two
of your favorite childhood activities? Schedule these into your
week. You deserve this "time out" from your overwhelming grief.

93.

KNOW THAT IT'S NATURAL TO RETHINK DEATH

"Confusion is the door that wisdom comes in through."
— Unknown

- The death of a child, at any age, changes the way in which we think about death. It changes how we think about our own death, the death of our own parents, and of our other children.

- Most bereaved parents do not fear death. Some have shared that they have a feeling of looking forward to dying because they are hopeful they will be reunited with their precious child. If you feel this way, it doesn't mean you are suicidal. It means that you long to be in the presence of your child.

- Passing thoughts of suicide are something many bereaved parents experience. Many say that they feel a desire to die, especially in the early days and weeks immediately after the death. This feeling usually wanes after a few weeks. If you have suicidal thoughts that do not subside or that seem very intense or constant, please get professional support immediately to help you find ways to survive the dark moments. If you are in need of immediate support, contact the 24-hour, toll-free National Suicide Prevention Lifeline at 800-273-8255 for help.

- As you continue on this grief journey, you may also find yourself thinking differently about subsequent deaths in the family. It is natural for bereaved parents to feel comforted by the fact that when someone else in the family dies, this person is now there to be with and watch over their child. So deaths of grandparents or others may offer reassurance in ways that others may not understand.

CARPE DIEM

Consider how you used to feel about death before your baby's death and how you feel about it now. How do you make sense of this difference? Is your changed thinking about death changing the way you are choosing to live your life?

94.

TALK TO SOMEONE ABOUT THE AFTERLIFE

*"That's what heaven is. You get to make
sense of your yesterdays."*
— Mitch Albom

- Depending on your spiritual beliefs, you may or may not believe in heaven per se, but if you are like most bereaved parents, you probably have some thoughts and feelings about what happens after death. If you have not thought about this much before, now that your baby has died it may be weighing more heavily on your mind.

- Of course there is no "right" answer as to whether or not there is a heaven or a place our spirits travel after they leave our physical bodies. There is only your answer.

- To explore your answer, it's important to have someone to listen to your thoughts. Do you have someone who can be a sounding board on this important issue? Are you willing to talk to your partner or kids about this?

- Some religions emphasize that death should be an event of celebration because it leads to eternal life. If this is your belief, perhaps this offers you a sense of comfort and peace that your baby is OK or in the arms of her maker. Even if you believe this to be true, you will still find that you need to mourn and embrace the reality that your baby is not here on earth with you.

CARPE DIEM

Write a description about or sketch a drawing of what you envision heaven to be. Be sure to include what you see your baby doing there. Perhaps this is something you and your spouse and kids can do together, as a family, so that you can all openly communicate about your beliefs about the baby's journey after death.

95.

REUNITE AND RECONNECT

"Nothing is more important than reconnecting with your bliss. Nothing is as rich. Nothing is more real."
— Deepak Chopra

• Throughout our lives, we often lose contact with the people who've touched us, helped us grow in some way, or made us feel loved and valued.

• Experiencing a tragic loss can make us realize that keeping in touch with people who bring a smile to our face is well worth the effort it takes.

• Whom have you loved or admired but haven't spoken with for a long time? Is there a mentor, a teacher, a childhood friend, or a previous neighbor that you have disconnected with over the years?

• Think about a person who made a difference in your life and take a moment to find a way to reconnect with her. Send her a Facebook message, drop a card in the mail, buy her a small gift, write an email, shoot her a text. Try to be open with her about what prompted you to reconnect and why she has been on your mind during this time of tremendous sadness in your life.

CARPE DIEM

Spend time today adding friends to your Facebook or LinkedIn pages. Find friends to follow on Twitter or Instagram that you haven't connected with in a while. Reconnecting with people you have lost touch with and re-inviting them into your life in small ways could be helpful. Perhaps it's a person from your past who will "get" what you are experiencing and turn out to be the best companion to you in grief.

96.

REMEMBER OTHERS WHO HAD A RELATIONSHIP WITH YOUR BABY

"To us, family means putting your arms around each other and being there."

— Barbara Bush

- Others around you are, in all likelihood, feeling a similar pain. Your other children, your partner, your parents, and your other family members are on their own grief journeys. Recognizing this is important. Here are a few ideas on what to do knowing that others are grieving around you:

  - Grieving children, especially, need our love and attention. If you have other children, help them find ways to actively mourn the death of their infant brother or sister. Invite them to talk about the baby, use the baby's name, and ask about the baby's death. It may surprise you to know what this loss is like through their eyes.
  - Is there someone outside of the inner circle of mourners who may also be struggling with this death? Your close friend who also lost a baby at birth or your obstetrician? Perhaps you could leave a voicemail or write a card acknowledging the love and friendship given during your pregnancy.
  - The grief of grandparents is often overlooked following stillbirth. Your parents are grieving for you as much as they are grieving for your baby's death. Let them know that you can see they are grieving and that getting support is a good thing. Though you may not be able to be there for them right now, know that their hearts have also been broken wide open by this loss.

CARPE DIEM

Create a family tree on the computer or by hand in memory of your baby. The tree will help you see all of the people who were connected to your child. Perhaps you can invite each person to contribute a sentence about how they felt connected to the baby that could become a part of this memory piece.

97.

RECONFIGURE YOUR LIFE

*"It is only possible to live happily ever
after on a day-to-day basis."*
— Margaret Bonnano

- When death enters our life in some form, it has a way of making us rethink the way we prioritize our days, interact with others, and spend our time. The death of a child, in particular, tends to awaken parents to what is truly meaningful and worthwhile in life.

- Have you considered what you give priority to? What gives your life meaning? Who are the people you want to spend time with? What are the activities you want to spend your valuable time doing? What doesn't give your life meaning that you still spend time on? What steps do you need to take to spend more of your time on the aspects of life that bring you a sense of meaning, purpose, and satisfaction?

- Now may be the time to reconfigure your life. After loss, we are less fearful and doubtful about our ability to reconfigure. Some parents change careers, go back to school, begin volunteering, start a non-profit, reach out to others through a blog, or focus their time on deepening their relationship with their surviving children.

- Many grieving parents talk about how they can no longer tolerate being around people who come across as shallow, egocentric, or mean-spirited. It's OK to let friendships that are not serving you well to come to an end. Instead, use your energy and time connecting with people who share your new outlook on living a meaningful life.

CARPE DIEM

Happiness is something everyone seems to be searching for. Do you know happiness when it's in front of you? Take a moment to make a list of what you see everyday that could be included under Happiness in the dictionary. Fill in this sentence so that you can begin to give some of your attention to thoughts outside of this loss.

Happiness is…

98.

BE PURPOSEFUL IN
EVERYTHING YOU DO

"Chase away sorrow by living."
— Melissa Marr

- Do you believe that you can make things happen by first creating them in your mind? The "Law of Attraction" (as it is sometimes called) has gained a lot of attention over the past several years.

- If you believe that what you focus on will grow, why not do more things "on purpose" so that you create the life you most desire?

- The life you desire right now, of course, probably includes having your baby back in your arms. Knowing that this is not possible, what intention could you set that allows you to experience something of the love, joy, and peace that holding your baby would bring you right now?

- For example, what if you lived with one of the following intentions over the next week?

I intend to wake up and teach something new to a child every day.

Today, I will set my intention to hold a child's hand or give her a hug so that she feels loved.

My intention for the day will be to be direct and honest with everyone I see about what I need from them as I mourn the loss of my baby.

- With a daily intention you will bring awareness into all of your interactions. Your intentional thoughts will create intentional actions. When you do this, you will experience a sense of control over at least some aspects of your destiny.

CARPE DIEM

Today set your intention for the coming month. With what attitude do you intend to wake up and enter the day? How do you intend to mourn so that you can learn to love and live well again?

99.

ALLOW YOURSELF TO BE "THANKFUL" WHEN YOU ARE READY

*"The difficulties of life are intended to
make us better, not bitter."*

— Unknown

- If you feel some resentment toward other parents, particularly in the early days and weeks after the death, know that this is natural. It is difficult to be in such pain and witness others living happily, sharing life with their children and families. You may feel resentful of other parents with newborns. After all, their child is alive and well. They had a normal, healthy pregnancy that went as it was supposed to. How unfair this seems. Why did this happen to you and not them?

- While you may appreciate others trying to connect and offer their condolences, you may not feel a sense of being "thankful" right now. Writing thank you cards may seem like the last thing you want to do. Enlist the help of someone else to keep track of phone calls, cards, flowers, etc. Put them in charge of sending thank you notes and following up with people who are offering support. Months and years from now you may take comfort in knowing you did.

- It is also OK to wait to say "thank you" if this helps you to survive. Your self has been assaulted and you need to focus on tending to the wounds right now. Over time, as the pain dissipates, you will be able to express your appreciation more honestly with others.

CARPE DIEM

Send a thank you card to yourself. Identify what you have
been doing to take care of you during this journey. Write what
you appreciate about how you've handled certain parts of this
experience. Offer yourself this moment of gratitude.

100.

EMBRACE YOUR TRANSFORMATION

"Sometimes a breakdown can be the beginning of a kind of breakthrough, a way of living in advance through a trauma that prepares you for a future of radical transformation."

— Cherrie Moraga

- You may find that you are changing emotionally and spiritually as a result of your grief journey. It may feel as if your insides have been shaken up or torn apart and that slowly they are falling back into different places. Your grief journey may be completely transforming, altering what once was into something strange and altogether new.

- Many grieving parents emerge from the early years of grief as stronger, more anchored people. Perhaps you are more assertive and apt to say what you really believe. Maybe you wear fewer masks and can be more of your true self in the presence of others. After such a devastating life loss, many parents don't give so much attention to meaningless things in life and know what truly matters day to day. It may feel as if you survived the worst life has to offer, so anything still to come cannot be so bad.

- What's more, as a bereaved parent perhaps you may have discovered the depths of your compassion for others, compassion you were unaware was a part of you. Don't be surprised if you find yourself volunteering, engaged in random acts of daily kindness, or more emotionally and spiritually attuned to others.

CARPE DIEM

Take a moment to write down what kind of transformations you have noticed in yourself since your baby died. Have you also noticed that your partner is transforming, and how do you feel about the transformations occurring?

A FINAL WORD

"But grief still has to be worked through. It is like walking through water. Sometimes there is an enormous breaker that knocks me down. Sometimes there is a sudden and fierce squall. But I know that many waters cannot quench love, neither can the floods drown it."

- Madeleine L'Engle, *Two-Part Intervention: The Story of a Marriage*

As you know, you are a different person than you were before your precious baby died. You have been knocked down, but not knocked out. You have been hurt, but not defeated.

In the beginning of this book we wrote, "Yes, you have a broken heart. We truly believe that acknowledging, and your heart is broken is the beginning of your healing. As you experience the pain of your loss—gently opening, acknowledging, and allowing—the suffering it has wrought diminishes but never completely vanishes." It's true—in loving your precious child, you opened yourself to life's greatest hurt, but also to life's greatest love.

Grieving parents like Lori-Ann Huot and Lori Esteve, both of whom experienced stillbirth and now lead organizations that help other grieving families after stillbirth, have taught us so much.

Grieving parents have taught us to slow down, to enjoy the moment, to find hidden treasures everywhere—a beautiful sunrise, a flower in bloom, a hike in the woods, a friend's gentle touch, a child's smile.

Grieving parents have taught us that there is so much to learn about ourselves and the world around us. They have taught us to live fully in the present while remembering our past and embracing our future.

Grieving parents have taught us to be open to giving and receiving love. They have taught us to seek a sense of belonging, a sense of meaning, a sense of purpose both in our life's work and in our relationships with family and friends. They have taught us there are magic and miracles in loving and being loved.

Most important, grieving parents have taught us so very much about what it means to love a child. Their lessons have permeated our souls and our ways of being with our own children.

Thank you to Lori and Lori for reviewing this manuscript and giving us their insightful feedback.

We often say that to mourn well is to live and love well again. Will you truly live or will you merely exist? Choosing to mourn openly, honestly, and authentically is, ultimately, to choose life and to discover hope, which is an expectation of a good that is yet to be.

Choose hope. Choose life. Godspeed.

RESOURCES

**Angel Whispers Baby Loss Support Program
(www.angelwhispers.ca/angelwhispers)**
Angel Whispers provides support and programs for parents who
have lost a baby shortly after birth, during pregnancy, miscarriage,
or stillbirth. They offer a quarterly newsletter as well as care
packages and birth certificate keepsakes.

**The Center for Loss in Multiple Birth (CLIMB), Inc.
(www.climb-support.org)**
This site was developed by and for parents throughout the United
States, Canada, and beyond who have experienced the death of one
or more children during a multiple pregnancy, the birthing process,
or in early infancy.

First Candle (www.firstcandle.org)
This site is dedicated to helping parents cope after the death of their
baby from SIDS, stillbirth, and other infant death.

HAND: Helping After Neonatal Death (www.handonline.org)
HAND, which stands for Helping After Neonatal Death, is a
nonprofit, volunteer group that provides support and information
to bereaved parents, their families, and friends following a
miscarriage, stillbirth, or newborn death.

Heavenly Angels in Need (www.heavenlyangelsinneed.com)
This agency provides burial items for your precious baby as well as
memory boxes free to grieving families.

Honored Babies (www.HonoredBabies.org)
A supportive site for parents whose babies have died due to
miscarriage, ectopic pregnancy, stillbirth, neonatal death, infancy
death, and/or pregnancy termination). On this site you will find
online memorials, online support group email lists (there's also one
for grandmothers), and a place to share your story.

Hygeia (www.hygeiafoundation.org)

Hygeia Foundation for Perinatal Loss and Bereavement, Inc.'s mission is to provide support during the painful experience of grief after the loss of a pregnancy or newborn child. Included are a resource center, poetry, memories and mementos, and stories.

Infants Remembered In Silence, Inc. (IRIS) (www.irisremembers.com)

IRIS was founded in 1987 and works with bereaved parents, families, and friends who have had an early pregnancy death, stillbirth, neonatal death, or a child die from birth defects, illness, accidents, and all other forms of infant and/or early childhood death.

MISS Foundation (www.misschildren.org)

The mission of MISS is to allow a safe haven for parents to share their grief after the death of a child. MISS provides support to parents enduring the tragedy of stillbirth, neonatal death, and infant death from any cause including SIDS and congenital anomalies.

Father's Page (www.missfoundation.org/support/articles/dads)

From the MISS site, just for dads.

Missing GRACE Organization (www.missinggrace.org)

The Missing GRACE Organization helps families on their journey through pregnancy and infant loss, infertility, and adoption. Provides support and resources to aid parents as they grieve, restore, arise, commemorate, and educate.

Mommies Enduring Neonatal Death (www.mend.org)

M.E.N.D. is a Christian nonprofit whose purpose is to reach out to those who have lost a child due to miscarriage, stillbirth, or early infant death and offer a way to share experiences and information through meetings, a bi-monthly newsletter, and website.

A Place to Remember (www.aplacetoremember.com)
A site committed to publishing and providing support materials and resources for those who have been touched by a crisis in pregnancy or the death of a baby.

Remembered Forever (www.remembered-forever.org)
This site offers users the chance to create a personalized online memorial for their lost loved ones. You can add photos, memories, videos, tributes, and stories as well as light virtual candles in remembrance.

S.O.B.B.S. (Stories of Babies Born Still) (www.facebook.com/groups/SOBBS)
This Facebook group is dedicated to supporting and educating families grieving a stillbirth.

SPALS: Subsequent Pregnancy After Loss (www.spals.com)
SPALS is a warm and compassionate group of people who have experienced the loss of a child due to miscarriage, selective termination, stillbirth, neonatal death, sudden infant death, or accidental death.

Stillbirthday (www.stillbirthday.com/bereavement-blogs/)
A site dedicated to helping you celebrate your child's day of birth. This site includes a supportive blog, a newsletter for parents, and information on other resources available for parents grieving the death of their stillborn baby.

Stillborn Angels Memory (www.stillborn-angels.memory-of.com)
A site that allows you to post pictures of your precious baby, leave messages of hope to your partner or other parents, and to light candles in memory of your baby.

THE MOURNER'S CODE

Ten Self-Compassionate Principles

Though you should reach out to others as you journey through grief, you should not feel obligated to accept the unhelpful responses you may receive from some people. You are the one who is grieving, and as such, you have certain "rights" no one should try to take away from you.

The following list is intended both to empower you to heal and to decide how others can and cannot help. This is not to discourage you from reaching out to others for help, but rather to assist you in distinguishing useful responses from hurtful ones.

1. **You have the right to experience your own unique grief.** No one else will grieve in exactly the same way you do. So, when you turn to others for help, don't allow them to tell you what you should or should not be feeling.

2. **You have the right to talk about your grief.** Talking about your grief will help you heal. Seek out others who will allow you to talk as much as you want, as often as you want, about your grief. If at times you don't feel like talking, you also have the right to be silent.

3. **You have the right to feel a multitude of emotions.** Confusion, numbness, disorientation, fear, guilt, and relief are just a few of the emotions you might feel as part of your grief journey. Others may try to tell you that feeling angry, for example, is wrong. Don't take these judgmental responses to heart. Instead, find listeners who will accept your feelings without condition.

4. **You have the right to be tolerant of your physical and emotional limits.** Your feelings of loss and sadness will probably leave you feeling fatigued. Respect what your body and mind are telling you. Get daily rest. Eat balanced meals. And don't

allow others to push you into doing things you don't feel ready to do.

5. **You have the right to experience "griefbursts."** Sometimes, out of nowhere, a powerful surge of grief may overcome you. This can be frightening, but it is normal and natural. Find someone who understands and will let you talk it out.

6. **You have the right to make use of ritual.** The funeral ritual does more than acknowledge the death of someone loved. It helps provide you with the support of caring people. More importantly, the funeral is a way for you to mourn. If others tell you the funeral or other healing rituals such as these are silly or unnecessary, don't listen.

7. **You have the right to embrace your spirituality.** If faith is a part of your life, express it in ways that seem appropriate to you. Allow yourself to be around people who understand and support your religious beliefs. If you feel angry at God, find someone to talk with who won't be critical of your feelings of hurt and abandonment.

8. **You have the right to search for meaning.** You may find yourself asking, "Why did he or she die? Why this way? Why now?" Some of your questions may have answers, but some may not. And watch out for the clichéd responses some people may give you. Comments like, "It was God's will" or "Think of what you have to be thankful for" are not helpful and you do not have to accept them.

9. **You have the right to treasure your memories.** Memories are one of the best legacies that exist after the death of someone loved. You will always remember. Instead of ignoring your memories, find others with whom you can share them.

10. **You have the right to move toward your grief and heal.** Reconciling your grief will not happen quickly. Remember, grief is a process, not an event. Be patient and tolerant with yourself and avoid people who are impatient and intolerant with you. Neither you nor those around you must forget that the death of someone loved changes your life forever.

WANTED:
YOUR IDEAS FOR HEALING
AFTER STILLBIRTH

Please help us write the next edition of this book. We will plan to update and rewrite this book every few years. For this reason we would really like to hear from you. Please write and let us know about your experience with this book.

If an Idea is particularly helpful to you, let us know. Better yet, send us an Idea you have that you think other fellow mourners might find helpful. When you write to us, you are "helping us help others" and inspiring us to be more effective grief companions, authors, and educators.

Thank you for your help. Please write to us at:

Center for Loss and Life Transition
3735 Broken Bow Road
Fort Collins, CO 80526
Or email us at DrWolfelt@centerforloss.com or go to this website, www.centerforloss.com.

My idea:

_____

_____

_____

_____

_____

My name and mailing address:

_____

_____

_____

ALSO BY ALAN WOLFELT

Understanding Your Grief

Ten Essential Touchstones for Finding Hope and Healing Your Heart

One of North America's leading grief educators, Dr. Alan Wolfelt has written many books about healing in grief. This book is his most comprehensive, covering the essential lessons that mourners have taught him in his three decades of working with the bereaved.

In compassionate, down-to-earth language, *Understanding Your Grief* describes ten touchstones—or trail markers—that are essential physical, emotional, cognitive, social, and spiritual signs for mourners to look for on their journey through grief.

The Ten Essential Touchstones:

1. Open to the presence of your loss.
2. Dispel misconceptions about grief.
3. Embrace the uniqueness of your grief.
4. Explore what you might experience.
5. Recognize you are not crazy.
6. Understand the six needs of mourning.
7. Nurture yourself.
8. Reach out for help.
9. Seek reconciliation, not resolution.
10. Appreciate your transformation.

Think of your grief as a wilderness—a vast, inhospitable forest. You must journey through this wilderness. To find your way out, you must become acquainted with its terrain and learn to follow the sometimes hard-to-find trail that leads to healing. In the wilderness of your grief, the touchstones are your trail markers. They are the signs that let you know you are on the right path. When you learn to identify and rely on the touchstones, you will find your way to hope and healing.

ISBN 978-1-879651-35-7 • 176 pages • softcover • $14.95

Companion
PRESS

All Dr. Wolfelt's publications can be ordered by mail from:
Companion Press
3735 Broken Bow Road
Fort Collins, CO 80526
(970) 226-6050
www.centerforloss.com

ALSO BY ALAN WOLFELT

Healing Your Grieving Heart for Kids
100 Practical Ideas

Healing Your Grieving Heart for Kids is for young and middle readers (6-12 year-olds) grieving the death of someone loved. The text is simple and straightforward, teaching children about grief and affirming that their thoughts and feelings are not only normal but necessary.

ISBN 978-1-879651-27-2 • 128 pages • softcover • $11.95

Companion
P R E S S

All Dr. Wolfelt's publications can be ordered by mail from:
Companion Press
3735 Broken Bow Road
Fort Collins, CO 80526
(970) 226-6050
www.centerforloss.com

ALSO BY ALAN WOLFELT

Healing Your Grieving Heart for Teens

100 Practical Ideas

In this compassionate book for grieving teenagers, Dr. Wolfelt speaks honestly and straightforwardly to teens, affirming their thoughts and feelings and giving them dozens of teen-friendly ideas for understanding and coping with their grief.

ISBN 978-1-879651-23-4 • 128 pages • softcover • $11.95

Companion
PRESS

All Dr. Wolfelt's publications can be ordered by mail from:
Companion Press
3735 Broken Bow Road
Fort Collins, CO 80526
(970) 226-6050
www.centerforloss.com